LIBRARY OF CLASSICS

THE GREATEST THING IN THE WORLD

by

HENRY DRUMMOND

With Introduction by
J. Y. SIMPSON

LONDON AND GLASGOW
COLLINS CLEAR-TYPE PRESS

CONTENTS

Part One

Part Two

INTRODUCTION

HENRY DRUMMOND was born at Stirling on the
17th of August, 1851 ; he died at Tunbridge Wells
on March 11th, 1897. Consequently his life, in
the maturity of its powers, was lived through a
most distinctive period—the last quarter of last
century—when the full impact of the truth that
was in Darwin was rapidly being felt far beyond
the narrow scientific area of its first dominance,
under the sledge-hammer blows of a Huxley or
the more overwhelming torrent of the Spencerian
philosophy. The noble if placid orthodoxy of the
greater Victorian poets notwithstanding, a ferment
was at work in the minds of many of the younger
generation, which in some cases resolved itself
into a struggle between loyalty to an old theology
or to a new science that were felt to be incompatible
with one another. Realising the basal correspon-
dences and unity of the truth which could be
reached along the various highways of Revelation,
Henry Drummond, with an inherited love for,
and broadly developed interest in, Natural Science,
strove to convey to others those glimpses of a

wider outlook and flashes from a penetrative insight that had cheered and illumined his own too solitary path. To what an extent he had met a need of his generation may be gathered from the fact that the British sales of one of his larger works,—*Natural Law in the Spiritual World*— reached something like 130,000 copies, whilst of the addresses here published, that one which gives title to the volume had in his lifetime a circulation of 350,000 in booklet form. His writings provoked criticism in many undiscerning quarters, but it is noteworthy that one of the most distinguished of his critics, long years after, made public avowal of how completely he had failed to gauge the need for, or estimate the value of, the kind of work, viz., that on the relations of scientific and religious thought, done by Drummond. It is a need that has only become more clamant with the passage of the years.

Under the moulding influence of an ideal home life, Henry Drummond passed by way of Edinburgh University, which he entered at the age of fifteen, into New College, Edinburgh, although with no very clear idea as to how the " call " to religious service which had led him thither, might eventually be responded to in his particular case. At no time, apparently, had he ever thought of the active ministry, and his interest in his scientific studies had never slackened. The natural bent of his mind towards preoccupation with the relations of scientific and religious thought was seen in the subjects that were selected by him for class or Debating Society essays during his student days, as e.g. the " Six Days of Creation " ; " Was the Deluge Partial ? " ; " The Doctrine of Creation." Then, in the third winter of his theological studies, he was swept into the current of the great Mission conducted by Messrs. Moody and Sankey in Great Britain during 1873–1875. It was an experience in which he found himself, and in which men began to realise his extraordinary powers of expression and appeal. " There's nobody in the world like Drummond for interesting young men," Mr. Moody had said; " set him to talk to a lot of 'em, and he'll just crop 'em in in five minutes." The Mission ended, he returned after two years' absence to the class-room benches, and quietly resumed his student place as if nothing had happened. Yet very much had happened, for while in the midst of the Mission he could say that " underlying my scientific studies and everything else, there has been this one settled conviction all these years—that the only life which to me would seem at all worth living would be a life of evangelistic work," a fuller experience had shown him that " the great thing is to *live* rather than to *work*," and that the immediate business for him now was in quietness and confidence to prepare himself spiritually for what he had no doubt would be made clear as God's purpose in life for him.

It is out of this background of sincere longing to discover the Will of God for himself that the addresses constituting the second part of this volume take their origin. Doubtless first given during his work with the American evangelists, they took later shape as addresses delivered during the winter of 1876–1877 in the Barclay Church, Edinburgh, where he had undertaken an assistantship. Although never prepared by him for publication, they were included along with others in a volume entitled *The Ideal Life*, issued after his death in 1897. This particular series on " The Will of God " as thus published was incomplete, and attention is drawn to the fact that the address entitled "God's will—the Christian's Aim," is now presented for the first time. It is particularly interesting as evidence of Henry Drummond's singular power of sympathetically imagining and describing a situation.

Very soon his way became clear before him. In

the autumn of 1877 he applied for the vacant lectureship on Natural Science in the Free Church College, Glasgow, and helped largely by a very commendatory testimonial from Sir Archibald Geikie, whom he later accompanied on a geological expedition to the Rocky Mountains, was elected to the post. Yet even with this definite demanding work in hand, he could not neglect the gift of evangelism that was in him. " I want a quiet mission somewhere," he wrote, " entry immediate and self-contained." It was his artisan audiences in Possil Park, Glasgow, who first heard the addresses that were afterwards collected and published as *Natural Law in the Spiritual World*. When, as the result of his work, the mission at Possil Park was made into a full charge, Henry Drummond retired from that post, and an ordained minister was appointed in his place. On his return from Africa in the spring of 1884 his lectureship, to which he had been re-appointed year by year, was raised to the status of a Chair through the vision and generosity of Mr. James Stevenson of Hailie, and he, unruffled by the rapidly mounting sales of his now famous book and the growing requests of those who sought spiritual counsel from him, was unanimously elected to the post by the General Assembly of his Church. His inaugural lecture on

" The Contribution of Science to Christianity,"
when published later, added greatly to his reputation.

The year 1885 is still remembered by an older
generation as the commencement of the long and
happy association of Henry Drummond with the
student life of Edinburgh University.   In the
autumn of 1884 the student world of Great Britain
was stirred by the news that Stanley Smith and
C. T. Studd, two brilliant Cambridge athletes, had
resolved, along with five of their college friends,
to devote themselves to mission work in China.
Previous to their departure, the two leaders paid
a series of farewell visits to various other Universities, and made such a deep impression in Edinburgh that they were invited to return if possible,
which they did, within two months' time.   The
results were so profoundly moving that the local
leaders felt that the work must be continued.   Now
it happened that in between the two visits of the
Cambridge volunteers, Professor Drummond had
delivered the annual lecture to the Christian
Medical Association of Edinburgh University,
taking as his subject " The Contribution of Science
to Christianity."   After that evening, when over
four hundred men were captured by his presen-
tation of old truth in a new light, it was not

difficult to know who should be invited to carry on the work. Most fortunately he accepted the invitation, and for ten years, until he was stricken by the illness which proved fatal, he addressed meetings of Edinburgh University students in the Oddfellows' Hall for from four to six Sundays every spring. Of those who assisted him most, probably least will ever be known. The earlier years were particularly memorable, for small deputations of the men headed by a professor or lecturer, visited the other Scottish Universities in turn, where, at meetings recognised by the local teaching staff, Christian Associations were formed, and the religious life of the University quickened. The resulting Holiday Mission, carefully organised under Drummond's immediate supervision, took groups of students to other towns and villages, and it is noteworthy that he made it a rule on all these occasions that the student members of the deputations should, so far as they went beyond describing the Edinburgh work, confine themselves merely to testifying to some truth that they had made their own by personal experience. In time news of the work reached far beyond Great Britain. As a result, on two occasions in the United States, in Australia, and on the Continent, Henry Drummond went by invitation from University to

University and College to College, sometimes accompanied by a representative deputation of Edinburgh professors or students, proclaiming the truth as he had come to see it. Out of this background, as also in connection with two series of meetings which he addressed in Grosvenor House, London, on the informal invitation of the Marquis and Marchioness of Aberdeen with the cordial co-operation of the then Duke of Westminster, came the addresses printed in the earlier section of this volume. There are those who still remember the thrill with which they first heard the outlines of the address on Love at a Northfield Conference, U.S.A., in the summer of 1887, although it had certainly been given some four years earlier at a mission station service in Central Africa.

It will be at once apparent, from internal evidence alone, that the group of addresses beginning with this one, best known of all, on " The Greatest Thing in the World," is, as a whole, the work of his maturer years. To few men of science is it given to write with clarity and distinction. From an early period Henry Drummond had practised writing, and in his later years became almost fastidious about phrasing and expression. In particular he would insist on the careful selection of adjectives, a part of speech which he considered to be especially determinative of the care that a writer put into his work. So it is not surprising to learn that the original Introduction to *The Ascent of Man*, his greatest book, was, after being set up in type, entirely re-written and reduced in length as the result of a friendly criticism, or that he had a large first edition of one of his booklets suppressed just before publication, because he discovered a faulty paragraph in it at the last moment,—" a knot in the porridge " as he put it. Some may recall his mot, " A *Nineteenth Century* article should be written at least three times, once in simplicity, once in profundity, and once to make the profundity appear simplicity." Even more strongly he wrote to a young friend in 1895, " For your humility read Frederick Harrison's article in the October number of *The Nineteenth Century* on Ruskin as a Master of English Prose. After reading it you will wonder, as I did, however any of us have the face to print a line."

Concerning his message, the addresses speak for themselves. They are as vital and constraining to-day as when he first delivered them. They gripped men ; they changed lives, not for a day but for all time. " I continually meet men from the Edinburgh meetings, holding like limpets," he wrote in 1890, during his tour in Australia. And his influence abides. Enter the private office of the Chief Magistrate of our capital city and the first thing that catches your eye is an enlarged photograph of Henry Drummond, and it would not be difficult to name man after man at the top of his profession to-day who would admit that one of the greatest influences for good in his life under God was Henry Drummond. This man, with something of the cavalier about him,—the students most closely associated with him in his work invariably spoke of him as " The Prince,"— with his wonderful power of literary expression, fine distinction of mind, and above all that selfless redemptive note about his life which was its key-note, eludes all efforts at portrayal. But that which he was, which he had at heart, and which was continuously exemplified in his life, may be glimpsed anew and savingly realised by another generation through his words.

J. Y. SIMPSON.

PART ONE

I.

THE GREATEST THING IN THE WORLD

THOUGH I speak with the tongues of men and of angels, and have not Love, I am become as sounding brass, or a tinkling cymbal. And though I have the gift of prophecy, and understand all mysteries, and all knowledge ; and though I have all faith, so that I could remove mountains, and have not Love, I am nothing. And though I bestow all my goods to feed the poor, and though I give my body to be burned, and have not Love, it profiteth me nothing.

Love suffereth long, and is kind ;
Love envieth not ;
Love vaunteth not itself, is not puffed up,
Doth not behave itself unseemly,
Seeketh not her own,
Is not easily provoked,
Thinketh no evil ;
Rejoiceth not in iniquity, but rejoiceth in the truth ;
Beareth all things, believeth all things, hopeth all things, endureth all things.

Love never faileth : but whether there be prophecies, they shall fail ; whether there be tongues, they shall cease ; whether there be knowledge, it shall vanish away. For we know in part, and we prophesy in part. But when that which is perfect is come, then that which is in part shall be done away. When I was a child, I spake as a child, I understood as a child, I thought as a child : but when I became a man, I put away childish things. For now we see through a glass, darkly ; but then face to face : now I know in part ; but then shall I know even as also I am known. And now abideth faith, hope, Love, these three ; but the greatest of these is Love.—I COR. xiii.

THE GREATEST THING
IN THE WORLD

EVERY one has asked himself the great question of antiquity as of the modern world : What is the *summum bonum*—the supreme good ? You have life before you. Once only you can live it. What is the noblest object of desire, the supreme gift to covet ?

We have been accustomed to be told that the greatest thing in the religious world is Faith. That great word has been the key-note for centuries of the popular religion ; and we have easily learned to look upon it as the greatest thing in the world. Well, we are wrong. If we have been told that, we may miss the mark. I have taken you, in the chapter which I have just read, to Christianity at its source ; and .there we have seen, " The greatest of these is love." It is not an over-sight. Paul was speaking of faith just a moment before. He says, " If I have all faith, so that I can remove mountains, and have not love, I am nothing." So far from forgetting, he deliberately contrasts them, " Now abideth Faith, Hope,

Love," and without a moment's hesitation, the decision falls, "The greatest of these is Love."

And it is not prejudice. A man is apt to recommend to others his own strong point. Love was not Paul's strong point. The observing student can detect a beautiful tenderness growing and ripening all through his character as Paul gets old ; but the hand that wrote, "The greatest of these is love," when we meet it first, is stained with blood.

Nor is this letter to the Corinthians peculiar in singling out love as the *summum bonum.* The masterpieces of Christianity are agreed about it. Peter says, "Above all things have fervent love among yourselves." *Above all things.* And John goes farther, "God is love." And you remember the profound remark which Paul makes elsewhere, "Love is the fulfilling of the law." Did you ever think what he meant by that ? In those days men were working their passage to Heaven by keeping the Ten Commandments, and the hundred and ten other commandments which they had manufactured out of them. Christ said, I will show you a more simple way. If you do one thing, you will do these hundred and ten things, without ever thinking about them. If you love, you will unconsciously fulfil the whole law. And you can readily see for yourselves how that must be so. Take any of the commandments. " Thou shalt have no other gods before Me." If a man love God, you will not require to tell him that. Love is the fulfilling of that law. " Take not His name in vain." Would he ever dream of taking His name in vain if he loved Him ? " Remember the Sabbath day to keep it holy." Would he not be too glad to have one day in seven to dedicate more exclusively to the object of his affection ? Love would fulfil all these laws regarding God. And so, if he loved Man, you would never think of telling him to honour his father and mother. He could not do anything else. It would be preposterous to tell him not to kill. You could only insult him if you suggested that he should not steal—how could he steal from those he loved ? It would be superfluous to beg him not to bear false witness against his neighbour. If he loved him it would be the last thing he would do. And you would never dream of urging him not to covet what his neighbours had. He would rather they possessed it than himself. In this way " Love is the fulfilling of the law." It is the rule for fulfilling all rules, the new commandment for keeping all the old commandments, Christ's one secret of the Christian life.

Now Paul had learned that ; and in this noble

eulogy he has given us the most wonderful and original account extant of the *summum bonum*. We may divide it into three parts. In the beginning of the short chapter, we have Love *contrasted ;* in the heart of it, we have Love *analysed ;* towards the end we have Love *defended* as the supreme gift.

THE CONTRAST

PAUL begins by contrasting Love with other things that men in those days thought much of. I shall not attempt to go over those things in detail. Their inferiority is already obvious.

He contrasts it with eloquence. And what a noble gift it is, the power of playing upon the souls and wills of men, and rousing them to lofty purposes and holy deeds. Paul says, " If I speak with the tongues of men and of angels, and have not love, I am become as sounding brass, or a tinkling cymbal." And we all know why. We have all felt the brazenness of words without emotion, the hollowness, the unaccountable unpersuasiveness, of eloquence behind which lies no Love.

He contrasts it with prophecy. He contrasts

it with mysteries. He contrasts it with faith. He contrasts it with charity. Why is Love greater than faith ? Because the end is greater than the means. And why is it greater than charity ? Because the whole is greater than the part. Love is greater than faith, because the end is greater than the means. What is the use of having faith ? It is to connect the soul with God. And what is the object of connecting man with God ? That he may become like God. But God is Love. Hence Faith, the means, is in order to Love, the end. Love, therefore, obviously is greater than faith. It is greater than charity, again, because the whole is greater than a part. Charity is only a little bit of Love, one of the innumerable avenues of Love, and there may even be, and there is, a great deal of charity without Love. It is a very easy thing to toss a copper to a beggar in the street ; it is generally an easier thing than not to do it. Yet Love is just as often in the withholding. We purchase relief from the sympathetic feelings roused by the spectacle of misery, at the copper's cost. It is too cheap—too cheap for us, and often too dear for the beggar. If we really loved him we would either do more for him, or less.

Then Paul contrasts it with sacrifice and martyrdom. And I beg the little band of would-be

missionaries—and I have the honour to call some
of you by this name for the first time—to remember
that though you give your bodies to be burned,
and have not Love, it profits nothing—nothing !
You can take nothing greater to the heathen world
than the impress and reflection of the Love of
God upon your own character. That is the universal
language. It will take you years to speak in
Chinese, or in the dialects of India. From the day
you land, that language of Love, understood by all,
will be pouring forth its unconscious eloquence.
It is the man who is the missionary, it is not his
words. His character is his message. In the heart
of Africa, among the great Lakes, I have come across
black men and women who remembered the only
white man they ever saw before—David Living-
stone ; and as you cross his footsteps in that dark
continent, men's faces light up as they speak of the
kind Doctor who passed there years ago. They
could not understand him ; but they felt the Love
that beat in his heart. Take into your new sphere
of labour, where you also mean to lay down your
life, that simple charm, and your lifework must
succeed. You can take nothing greater, you need
take nothing less. It is not worth while going if
you take anything less. You may take every
accomplishment ; you may be braced for every

sacrifice ; but if you give your body to be burned, and have not Love, it will profit you and the cause of Christ *nothing*.

THE ANALYSIS

AFTER contrasting Love with these things, Paul in three verses, very short, gives us an amaz__g analysis of what this supreme thing is. I ask you to look at it. It is a compound thing, he tells us. It is like light. As you have seen a man of science take a beam of light and pass it through a crystal prism, as you have seen it come out on the other side of the prism broken up into its component colours—red, and blue, and yellow, and violet, and orange, and all the colours of the rainbow— so Paul passes this thing, Love, through the magnificent prism of his inspired intellect, and it comes out on the other side broken up into its elements. And in these few words we have what one might call the Spectrum of Love, the analysis of Love. Will you observe what its elements are ? Will you notice that they have common names ; that they are virtues which we hear about every day ; that they are things which can be practised by every man in every place in life ; and how, by a multitude of small things and ordinary virtues, the supreme thing, the *summum bonum*, is made up ?

The Spectrum of Love has nine ingredients :—

Patience . .	" Love suffereth long."
Kindness . .	" And is kind."
Generosity .	" Love envieth not."
Humility . .	" Love vaunteth not itself, is not puffed up."
Courtesy . .	" Doth not behave itself unseemly."
Unselfishness	" Seeketh not her own."
Good Temper	" Is not easily provoked."
Guilelessness .	" Thinketh no evil."
Sincerity . .	" Rejoiceth not in iniquity, but rejoiceth in the truth."

Patience ; kindness ; generosity ; humility ; courtesy ; unselfishness ; good temper ; guile-lessness ; sincerity—these make up the supreme gift, the stature of the perfect man. You will observe that all are in relation to men, in relation to life, in relation to the known to-day and the near to-morrow, and not to the unknown eternity. We hear much of love to God ; Christ spoke much of love to man. We make a great deal of peace with heaven ; Christ made much of peace on earth.

Religion is not a strange or added thing, but the inspiration of the secular life, the breathing of an eternal spirit through this temporal world. The supreme thing, in short, is not a thing at all, but the giving of a further finish to the multitudinous words and acts which make up the sum of every common day

There is no time to do more than make a passing note upon each of these ingredients. Love is *Patience*. This is the normal attitude of Love ; Love passive, Love waiting to begin ; not in a hurry ; calm ; ready to do its work when the summons comes, but meantime wearing the ornament of a meek and quiet spirit. Love suffers long ; beareth all things ; believeth all things ; hopeth all things. For Love understands, and therefore waits.

Kindness. Love active. Have you ever noticed how much of Christ's life was spent in doing kind things—in *merely* doing kind things ? Run over it with that in view, and you will find that He spent a great proportion of His time simply in making people happy, in doing good turns to people. There is only one thing greater than happiness in the world, and that is holiness ; and it is not in our keeping ; but what God *has* put in our power is the happiness of those about us, and that is largely to be secured by our being kind to them.

"The greatest thing," says some one, "a man can do for his Heavenly Father is to be kind to some of His other children." I wonder why it is that we are not all kinder than we are. How much the world needs it. How easily it is done. How instantaneously it acts. How infallibly it is re-membered. How superabundantly it pays itself back—for there is no debtor in the world so honour-able, so superbly honourable, as Love. "Love never faileth." Love is success, Love is happiness, Love is life. "Love, I say," with Browning, "is energy of Life."

"For life, with all it yields of joy and woe
   And hope and fear,
   Is just our chance o' the prize of learning love—
   How love might be, hath been indeed, and is."

Where Love is, God is. He that dwelleth in Love dwelleth in God. God is love. Therefore *love*. Without distinction, without calculation, without procrastination, love. Lavish it upon the poor, where it is very easy ; especially upon the rich, who often need it most ; most of all upon our equals, where it is very difficult, and for whom perhaps we each do least of all. There is a difference between *trying to please* and *giving pleasure*. Give pleasure. Lose no chance of giving pleasure. For that is the ceaseless and anonymous triumph of a truly loving spirit. " I will pass through this world but once. Any good thing therefore that I can do, or any kindness that I can show to any human being, let me do it now. Let me not defer it or neglect it, for I shall not pass this way again."

Generosity. " Love envieth not." This is Love in competition with others. Whenever you attempt a good work you will find other men doing the same kind of work, and probably doing it better. Envy them not. Envy is a feeling of ill-will to those who are in the same line as ourselves, a spirit of covetousness and detraction. How little Christian work even is a protection against un-Christian feeling. That most despicable of all the unworthy moods which cloud a Christian's soul assuredly waits for us on the threshold of every work, unless we are fortified with this grace of magnanimity. Only one thing truly need the Christian envy, the large, rich, generous soul which " envieth not."

And then, after having learned all that, you have to learn this further thing, *Humility*— to put a seal upon your lips and forget what you have done. After you have been kind, after Love has stolen forth into the world and done its beautiful work, go back into the shade again and say nothing about it. Love hides even from itself. Love waives even self-satisfaction. "Love vaunteth not itself, is not puffed up."

The fifth ingredient is a somewhat strange one to find in this *summum bonum : Courtesy*. This is Love in society, Love in relation to etiquette. "Love doth not behave itself unseemly." Politeness has been defined as love in trifles. Courtesy is said to be love in little things. And the one secret of politeness is to love. Love *cannot* behave itself unseemly. You can put the most untutored person into the highest society, and if they have a reservoir of love in their heart, they will not behave themselves unseemly. They simply cannot do it. Carlyle said of Robert Burns that there was no truer gentleman in Europe than the ploughman-poet. It was because he loved everything—the mouse, and the daisy, and all the things, great and small, that God had made. So with this simple passport he could mingle with any society, and enter courts and palaces from his little cottage on the banks of the Ayr. You know the meaning of the word " gentleman." It means a gentle man—a man who does things gently, with love. And that is the whole art and mystery of it. The gentle man cannot in the nature of things do an ungentle, an ungentlemanly thing. The ungentle soul, the inconsiderate, unsympathetic nature cannot do anything else. " Love doth not behave itself unseemly."

Unselfishness. " Love seeketh not her own." Observe : Seeketh not even that which is her own. In Britain the Englishman is devoted, and rightly, to his rights. But there come times when a man may exercise even the higher right of giving up his rights. Yet Paul does not summon us to give up our rights. Love strikes much deeper. It would have us not seek them at all, ignore them, eliminate the personal element altogether from our calculations. It is not hard to give up our rights. They are often external The difficult thing is to give up ourselves. The more difficult thing still is not to seek things for ourselves at all. After we have sought them, bought them, won them, deserved them, we have taken the cream off them for ourselves already. Little cross then, perhaps, to give them up. But not to seek them, to look every man not on his own things, but on the things of others—*id opus est.* " Seekest thou great things for thyself ? " said the prophet ; " *seek them not.*" Why ? Because there is no greatness in *things.* Things cannot be great. The only greatness is unselfish love. Even self-denial in itself is nothing, is almost a mistake. Only a great purpose or a mightier love can justify the waste. It is more difficult, I have said, not to seek our own at all, than, having sought it, to give it up. I must take that back. It is only true of a partly selfish heart. Nothing is a hardship to Love, and nothing is hard. I believe that Christ's yoke is easy. Christ's " yoke " is just His way of taking life. And I believe it is an easier way than any other. I believe it is a happier way than any other. The most obvious lesson in Christ's teaching is that there is no happiness in having and getting anything, but only in giving. I repeat, *there is no happiness in having, or in getting, but only in giving*. And half the world is on the wrong scent in the pursuit of happiness. They think it consists in having and getting, and in being served by others. It consists in giving and serving others. He that would be great among you, said Christ, let him serve. He that would be happy, let him remember that there is but one way—it is more blessed, it is more happy, to give than to receive.

The next ingredient is a very remarkable one : *Good Temper*. " Love is not easily provoked." Nothing could be more striking than to find this here. We are inclined to look upon bad temper as a very harmless weakness. We speak of it as a mere infirmity of nature, a family failing, a matter of temperament, not a thing to take into very serious account in estimating a man's character. And yet here, right in the heart of this analysis of love, it finds a place ; and the Bible again and again returns to condemn it as one of the most destructive elements in human nature.

The peculiarity of ill temper is that it is the vice of the virtuous. It is often the one blot on an otherwise noble character. You know men who are all but perfect, and women who would be entirely perfect, but for an easily ruffled, quick-tempered, or " touchy " disposition. This compatibility of ill temper with high moral character is one of the strangest and saddest problems of ethics. The truth is there are two great classes of sins—sins of the *Body*, and sins of the *Disposition*. The Prodigal Son may be taken as a type of the first, the Elder Brother of the second. Now society has no doubt whatever as to which of these is the worse. Its brands falls, without a challenge, upon the Prodigal. But are we right ? We have no balance to weigh one another's sins, and coarser and finer are but human words ; but faults in the higher nature may be less venial than those in the lower, and to the eye of Him who is Love, a sin against Love may seem a hundred times more base. No form of vice, not worldliness, not greed of gold, not drunkenness itself, does more to un-Christianise society than evil temper. For embittering life, for breaking up communities, for destroying the most sacred relationships, for devastating homes, for withering up men and women, for taking the bloom off childhood ; in short, for sheer gratuitous misery-producing power, this influence stands alone. Look at the Elder Brother, moral, hard-working, patient, dutiful—let him get all credit for his virtues—look at this man, this baby, sulking outside his own father's door. " He was angry," we read, " and would not go in." Look at the effect upon the father, upon the servants, upon the happiness of the guests. Judge of the effect upon the Prodigal—and how many prodigals are kept out of the Kingdom of God by the unlovely characters of those who profess to be inside ? Analyse, as a study in Temper, the thunder-cloud itself as it gathers upon the Elder Brother's brow. What is it made of ? Jealousy, anger, pride, uncharity, cruelty, self-righteousness, touchiness, doggedness, sullenness—these are the ingredients of this dark and loveless soul. In vary-ing proportions, also, these are the ingredients of all ill temper. Judge if such sins of the disposition are not worse to live in, and for others to live with, than sins of the body. Did Christ indeed not

answer the question Himself when He said, " I
say unto you, that the publicans and the harlots
go into the Kingdom of Heaven before you."
There is really no place in Heaven for a disposition
like this. A man with such a mood could only make
Heaven miserable for all the people in it. Except,
therefore, such a man be born again, he cannot, he
simply *cannot*, enter the Kingdom of Heaven. For
it is perfectly certain—and you will not misunderstand me—that to enter Heaven a man must take
it with him.

You will see then why Temper is significant.
It is not in what it is alone, but in what it reveals.
This is why I take the liberty now of speaking of it
with such unusual plainness. It is a test for love, a
symptom, a revelation of an unloving nature at
bottom. It is the intermittent fever which bespeaks
unintermittent disease within ; the occasional
bubble escaping to the surface which betrays some
rottenness underneath ; a sample of the most
hidden products of the soul dropped involuntarily
when off one's guard ; in a word, the lightning
form of a hundred hideous and un-Christian sins.
For a want of patience, a want of kindness, a
want of generosity, a want of courtesy, a want of
unselfishness, are all instantaneously symbolised
in one flash of Temper.

Hence it is not enough to deal with the Temper. We must go to the source, and change the inmost nature, and the angry humours will die away of themselves. Souls are made sweet not by taking the acid fluids out, but by putting something in— a great Love, a new Spirit, the Spirit of Christ. Christ, the Spirit of Christ, interpenetrating ours, sweetens, purifies, transforms all. This only can eradicate what is wrong, work a chemical change, renovate and regenerate, and rehabilitate the inner man. Will-power does not change men. Time does not change men. Christ does. Therefore " Let that mind be in you which was also in Christ Jesus." Some of us have not much time to lose. Remember, once more, that this is a matter of life or death. I cannot help speaking urgently, for myself, for yourselves. " Whoso shall offend one of these little ones, which believe in me, it were better for him that a millstone were hanged about his neck, and that he were drowned in the depth of the sea." That is to say, it is the deliberate verdict of the Lord Jesus that it is better not to live than not to love. *It is better not to live than not to love.*

Guilelessness and *Sincerity* may be dismissed almost with a word. Guilelessness is the grace for suspicious people. And the possession of it is the great secret of personal influence. You will find, if you think for a moment, that the people who influence you are people who believe in you. In an atmosphere of suspicion men shrivel up ; but in that atmosphere they expand, and find encouragement and educative fellowship. It is a wonderful thing that here and there in this hard, uncharitable world there should still be left a few rare souls who think no evil. This is the great unworldliness. Love " thinketh no evil," imputes no motive, sees the bright side, puts the best construction on every action. What a delightful state of mind to live in ! What a stimulus and benediction even to meet with it for a day ! To be trusted is to be saved. And if we try to influence or elevate others, we shall soon see that success is in proportion to their belief of our belief in them. For the respect of another is the first restoration of the self-respect a man has lost ; our ideal of what he is becomes to him the hope and pattern of what he may become.

"Love rejoiceth not in iniquity, but rejoiceth in the truth." I have called this *Sincerity* from the words rendered in the Authorised Version by " rejoiceth in the truth." And, certainly, were this the real translation, nothing could be more just. For he who loves will love Truth not less than men. He will rejoice in the Truth—rejoice not in what he has been taught to believe ; not in this

Church's doctrine or in that ; not in this ism or in that ism ; but " in *the Truth.*" He will accept only what is real ; he will strive to get at facts ; he will search for *Truth* with a humble and unbiased mind, and cherish whatever he finds at any sacrifice. But the more literal translation of the Revised Version calls for just such a sacrifice for truth's sake here. For what Paul really meant is, as we there read, " Rejoiceth not in unrighteousness, but rejoiceth with the truth," a quality which probably no one English word—and certainly not *Sincerity*— adequately defines. It includes, perhaps more strictly, the self-restraint which refuses to make capital out of others' faults ; the charity which delights not in exposing the weakness of others, but " covereth all things " ; the sincerity of purpose which endeavours to see things as they are, and rejoices to find them better than suspicion feared or calumny denounced.

So much for the analysis of Love. Now the business of our lives is to have these things fitted into our characters. That is the supreme work to which we need to address ourselves in this world, to learn Love. Is life not full of opportunities for learning Love ? Every man and woman every day has a thousand of them. The world is not a play-ground ; it is a school-room. Life is not a holiday, but an education. And the one eternal lesson for us all is *how better we can love*. What makes a man a good cricketer ? Practice. What makes a man a good artist, a good sculptor, a good musician ? Practice. What makes a man a good linguist, a good stenographer ? Practice. What makes a man a good man ? Practice. Nothing else. There is nothing capricious about religion. We do not get the soul in different ways, under different laws, from those in which we get the body and the mind. If a man does not exercise his arm he develops no biceps muscle ; and if a man does not exercise his soul, he acquires no muscle in his soul, no strength of character, no vigour of moral fibre, nor beauty of spiritual growth. Love is not a thing of enthusiastic emotion. It is a rich, strong, manly, vigorous expression of the whole round Christian character. —the Christ-like nature in its fullest development. And the constituents of this great character are only to be built up by ceaseless practice.

What was Christ doing in the carpenter's shop ? Practising. Though perfect, we read that He *learned* obedience, He *increased* in wisdom and in favour with God and man. Do not quarrel therefore with your lot in life. Do not complain of its never-ceasing cares, its petty environment, the vexations you have to stand, the small and sordid souls you have to live and work with. Above all, do not resent temptation ; do not be perplexed because it seems to thicken round you more and more, and ceases neither for effort nor for agony nor prayer. That is the practice which God appoints you ; and it is having its work in making you patient, and humble, and generous, and unselfish, and kind, and courteous Do not grudge the hand that is moulding the still too shapeless image within you. It is growing more beautiful though you see it not, and every touch of temptation may add to its perfection. Therefore keep in the midst of life. Do not isolate yourself. Be among men, and among things, and among troubles, and difficulties, and obstacles. You remember Goethe's words : *Es bildet ein Talent sich in der Stille, Doch ein Character in dem Strom der Welt*. " Talent develops itself in solitude ; character in the stream of life." Talent develops itself in solitude—the talent of prayer, of faith, of meditation, of seeing the unseen ; Character grows in the stream of the world's life. That chiefly is where men are to learn love.

How ? Now, how ? To make it easier, I have named a few of the elements of love. But these are only elements. Love itself can never be defined. Light is a something more than the sum of its

ingredients—a glowing, dazzling, tremulous ether.
And love is something more than all its elements—
a palpitating, quivering, sensitive, living thing.
By synthesis of all the colours, men can make
whiteness, they cannot make light. By synthesis
of all the virtues, men can make virtue, they cannot
make love. How then are we to have this transcendent living whole conveyed into our souls?
We brace our wills to secure it. We try to copy
those who have it. We lay down rules about it.
We watch. We pray. But these things alone will
not bring Love into our nature. Love is an *effect*.
And only as we fulfil the right condition can we
have the effect produced. Shall I tell you what the
cause is?

If you turn to the Revised Version of the First
Epistle of John you will find these words: "We
love, because He first loved us." "We love,"
not "We love *Him*. That is the way the old
Version has it, and it is quite wrong. "*We
love*—because He first loved us." Look at that
word "because." It is the *cause* of which I
have spoken. "*Because* He first loved us," the
effect follows that we love, we love Him, we love
all men. We cannot help it. Because He loved us,
we love, we love everybody. Our heart is slowly
changed. Contemplate the love of Christ, and you

will love. Stand before that mirror, reflect Christ's character, and you will be changed into the same image from tenderness to tenderness. There is no other way. You cannot love to order. You can only look at the lovely object, and fall in love with it, and grow into likeness to it And so look at this Perfect Character, this Perfect Life. Look at the great Sacrifice as He laid down Himself, all through life, and upon the Cross of Calvary ; and you must love Him. And loving Him, you must become like Him. Love begets love. It is a process of induction. Put a piece of iron in the presence of a magnetised body, and that piece of iron for a time becomes magnetised It is charged with an attractive force in the mere presence of the original force, and as long as you leave the two side by side, they are both magnets alike. Remain side by side with Him who loved us, and gave Himself for us, and you too will become a centre of power, a permanently attractive force ; and like Him you will draw all men unto you, like Him you will be drawn unto all men That is the inevitable effect of Love. Any man who fulfils that cause must have that effect produced in him. Try to give up the idea that religion comes to us by chance, or by mystery, or by caprice It comes to us by natural law. or by supernatural law, for all law is Divine. Edward Irving

went to see a dying boy once, and when he entered
the room he just put his hand on the sufferer's
head, and said, "My boy, God loves you," and
went away. And the boy started from his bed,
and called out to the people in the house, "God loves
me! God loves me!" It changed that boy. The
sense that God loved him overpowered him, melted
him down, and began the creating of a new heart
in him. And that is how the love of God melts
down the unlovely heart in man, and begets in
him the new creature, who is patient and humble and
gentle and unselfish. And there is no other way to
get it. There is no mystery about it. We love
others, we love everybody, we love our enemies,
because He first loved us.

THE DEFENCE

Now I have a closing sentence or two to add
about Paul's reason for singling out love as the
supreme possession. It is a very remarkable
reason. In a single word it is this : *it lasts*. "Love,"
urges Paul, "never faileth." Then he begins again
one of his marvellous lists of the great things of
the day, and exposes them one by one. He runs

over the things that men thought were going to last, and shows that they are all fleeting, temporary, passing away.

"Whether there be prophecies, they shall fail." It was the mother's ambition for her boy in those days that he should become a prophet. For hundreds of years God had never spoken by means of any prophet, and at that time the prophet was greater than the king. Men waited wistfully for another messenger to come, and hung upon his lips when he appeared as upon the very voice of God. Paul says, "Whether there be prophecies they shall fail." This Book is full of prophecies. One by one they have "failed"; that is, having been fulfilled their work is finished; they have nothing more to do now in the world except to feed a devout man's faith.

Then Paul talks about tongues. That was another thing that was greatly coveted. "Whether there be tongues, they shall cease." As we all know, many centuries have passed since tongues have been known in this world. They have ceased. Take it in any sense you like. Take it, for illustration merely as languages in general—a sense which was not in Paul's mind at all, and which though it cannot give us the specific lesson will point the general truth. Consider the words in which these chapters were written—Greek. It has gone. Take the Latin—the other great tongue of those days. It ceased long ago. Look at the Indian language. It is ceasing. The language of Wales, of Ireland, of the Scottish Highlands is dying before our eyes. The most popular book in the English tongue at the present time, except the Bible, is one of Dickens's works, his *Pickwick Papers*. It is largely written in the language of London street-life ; and experts assure us that in fifty years it will be unintelligible to the average English reader.

Then Paul goes farther, and with even greater boldness adds. " Whether there be knowledge, it shall vanish away." The wisdom of the ancients, where is it ? It is wholly gone. A schoolboy to-day knows more than Sir Isaac Newton knew. His knowledge has vanished away. You put yesterday's paper in the fire. Its knowledge has vanished away. You buy the old editions of the great encyclopædias for a few pence. Their knowledge has vanished away. Look how the coach has been superseded by the use of steam. Look how electricity has superseded that, and swept a hundred almost new inventions into oblivion. One of the greatest living authorities, Sir William Thomson, said the other day, " The steam-engine is passing away."

" Whether there be knowledge, it shall vanish away " At every workshop you will see, in the back yard, a heap of old iron, a few wheels, a few levers, a few cranks, broken and eaten with rust. Twenty years ago that was the pride of the city. Men flocked in from the country to see the great invention ; now it is superseded, its day is done. And all the boasted science and philosophy of this day will soon be old. But yesterday, in the University of Edinburgh, the greatest figure in the faculty was Sir James Simpson, the discoverer of chloroform. The other day his successor and nephew, Professor Simpson, was asked by the librarian of the University to go to the library and pick out the books on his subject that were no longer needed. And his reply to the librarian was this : " Take every text book that is more than ten years old, and put it down in the cellar." Sir James Simpson was a great authority only a few years ago : men came from all parts of the earth to consult him ; and almost the whole teaching of that time is consigned by the science of to-day to oblivion And in every branch of science it is the same. " Now we know in part. We see through a glass darkly."

Can you tell me anything that is going to last ? Many things Paul did not condescend to name.

He did not mention money, fortune, fame ; but he picked out the great things of his time, the things the best men thought had something in them, and brushed them peremptorily aside. Paul had no charge against these things in themselves. All he said about them was that they would not last. They were great things, but not supreme things. They were things beyond them. What we are stretches past what we do, beyond what we possess. Many things that men denounce as sins are not sins ; but they are temporary. And that is a favourite argument of the New Testament. John says of the world, not that it is wrong, but simply that it " passeth away." There is a great deal in the world that is delightful and beautiful ; there is a great deal in it that is great and engrossing ; but it will not last. All that is in the world, the lust of the eye, the lust of the flesh, and the pride of life, are but for a little while. Love not the world therefore. Nothing that it contains is worth the life and consecration of an immortal soul. The immortal soul must give itself to something that is immortal. And the only immortal things are these : " Now abideth faith, hope, love, but the greatest of these is love."

Some think the time will come when two of these three things will also pass away—faith into sight, hope into fruition. Paul does not say so. We know but little now about the conditions of the life that is to come. But what is certain is that Love must last. God, the Eternal God, is Love. Covet therefore that everlasting gift, that one thing which it is certain is going to stand, that one coinage which will be current in the Universe when all the other coinages of all the nations of the world shall be useless and unhonoured. You will give yourselves to many things, give yourselves first to Love. Hold things in their proportion. *Hold things in their proportion.* Let at least the first great object of our lives be to achieve the character defended in these words, the character,—and it is the character of Christ—which is built round Love.

I have said this thing is eternal. Did you ever notice how continually John associates love and faith with eternal life ? I was not told when I was a boy that " God so loved the world that He gave His only begotten Son, that whosoever believeth in Him should have everlasting life." What I was told, I remember, was, that God so loved the world that, if I trusted in Him, I was to have a thing called peace, or I was to have rest, or I was to have joy, or I was to have safety. But I had to find out for myself that whosoever trusteth in Him—that is, whosoever loveth

Him, for trust is only the avenue to Love—hath everlasting *life*. The Gospel offers a man life. Never offer men a thimbleful of Gospel. Do not offer them merely joy, or merely peace, or merely rest, or merely safety ; tell them how Christ came to give men a more abundant life than they have, a life abundant in love, and therefore abundant in salvation for themselves, and large in enterprise for the alleviation and redemption of the world. Then only can the Gospel take hold of the whole of a man, body, soul, and spirit, and give to each part of his nature its exercise and reward. Many of the current Gospels are addressed only to a part of man's nature. They offer peace, not life ; faith, not Love ; justification, not regeneration. And men slip back again from such religion because it has never really held them. Their nature was not all in it. It offered no deeper and gladder life-current than the life that was lived before. Surely it stands to reason that only a fuller love can compete with the love of the world.

To love abundantly is to live abundantly, and to love for ever is to live for ever. Hence, eternal life is inextricably bound up with love. We want to live for ever for the same reason that we want to live to-morrow. Why do you want to live to-morrow ? It is because there is some one who loves you, and whom you want to see to-morrow, and be with, and love back. There is no other reason why we should live on than that we love and are beloved. It is when a man has no one to love him that he commits suicide. So long as he has friends, those who love him and whom he loves, he will live ; because to live is to love. Be it but the love of a dog, it will keep him in life ; but let that go and he has no contact with life, no reason to live. The " energy of life " has failed. Eternal life also is to know God, and God is love. This is Christ's own definition. Ponder it. " This is life eternal, that they might know Thee the only true God, and Jesus Christ whom Thou hast sent." Love must be eternal. It is what God is. On the last analysis, then, love is Life. Love never faileth, and life never faileth, so long as there is love. That is the philosophy of what Paul is showing us ; the reason why in the nature of things Love should be the supreme thing—because it is going to last ; because in the nature of things it is an Eternal Life. That Life is a thing that we are living now, not that we get when we die ; that we shall have a poor chance of getting when we die unless we are living now. No worse fate can befall a man in this world than to live and grow old alone, unloving and un-loved. To be lost is to live in an unregenerate condition, loveless and unloved ; and to be saved is to love ; and he that dwelleth in love dwelleth already in God. For God is love.

Now I have all but finished. How many of you will join me in reading this chapter once a week for the next three months ? A man did that once and it changed his whole life. Will you do it ? It is for the greatest thing in the world. You might begin by reading it every day, especially the verses which describe the perfect character. " Love suffereth long, and is kind ; love envieth not ; love vaunteth not itself." Get these ingredients into your life. Then everything that you do is eternal. It is worth doing. It is worth giving time to. No man can become a saint in his sleep ; and to fulfil the condition required demands a certain amount of prayer and meditation and time, just as improvement in any direction, bodily or mental, requires preparation and care. Address yourself to that one thing ; at any cost have this transcendent character exchanged for yours. You will find as you look back upon your life that the moments that stand out, the moments when you have really lived, are the moments when you have done things in a spirit of love. As memory scans the past, above and beyond all the transitory pleasures of life, there leap forward those supreme hours when you have been enabled to do unnoticed kindnesses to those around about you, things too trifling to speak about, but which you feel have entered into your eternal life. I have seen almost all the beautiful things that God has made; I have enjoyed almost every pleasure that He has planned for man; and yet as I look back I see standing out above all the life that has gone four or five short experiences when the love of God reflected itself in some poor imitation, some small act of love of mine, and these seem to be the things which alone of all one's life abide. Everything else in all our lives is transitory. Every other good is visionary. But the acts of love which no man knows about, or can ever know about—they never fail.

In the Book of Matthew, where the Judgment Day is depicted for us in the imagery of One seated upon a throne and dividing the sheep from the goats, the test of a man then is not, "How have I believed?" but " How have I loved ? " The test of religion, the final test of religion, is not religiousness, but Love. I say the final test of religion at that great Day is not religiousness, but Love; not what I have done, not what I have believed, not what I have achieved, but how I have discharged the common charities of life. Sins of commission in that awful indictment are not even referred to. By what we have not done, *by sins of omission*, we are judged. It could not be otherwise. For the withholding of love is the negation of the spirit of Christ, the proof that we never knew Him, that for us He lived in vain. It means that He suggested nothing in all our thoughts, that He inspired nothing in all our lives, that we were not once near enough to Him to be seized with the spell of His compassion for the world. It means that :

> " I lived for myself, I thought for myself,
> For myself, and none beside—
> Just as if Jesus had never lived,
> As if He had never died."

It is the Son of *Man* before whom the nations of the world shall be gathered. It is in the presence of *Humanity* that we shall be charged. And the spectacle itself, the mere sight of it, will silently judge each one. Those will be there whom we have met and helped ; or there, the unpitied multitude whom we neglected or despised. No other Witness need be summoned. No other charge than loveless-ness shall be preferred. Be not deceived. The words which all of us shall one Day hear, sound not of theology but of life, not of churches and saints but of the hungry and the poor, not of creeds and doctrines but of shelter and clothing, not of Bibles and prayer-books but of cups of cold water in the name of Christ. Thank God the Christianity of to-day is coming nearer the world's need. Live to help that on. Thank God men know better, by a hairsbreadth, what religion is, what God is, who Christ is, where Christ is. Who is Christ? He who fed the hungry, clothed the naked, visited the sick. And where is Christ? Where?—whoso shall receive a little child in My name receiveth Me. And who are Christ's? Every one that loveth is born of God.

II.

THE
PROGRAMME OF CHRISTIANITY

To Preach Good Tidings unto the Meek :
To Bind up the Broken-Hearted :
To Proclaim Liberty to the Captives and the Opening
of the Prison to Them that are Bound :
To Proclaim the Acceptable Year of the Lord, and
the Day of Vengeance of our God :
To Comfort all that Mourn :
To Appoint unto them that Mourn in Zion :
To Give unto them—
Beauty for Ashes,
The Oil of Joy for Mourning,
The Garment of Praise for the Spirit of Heaviness.

THE
PROGRAMME OF CHRISTIANITY

" WHAT does God do all day ? " once asked a
little boy. One could wish that more grown-up
people would ask so very real a question. Unfortunately, most of us are not even boys in religious
intelligence, but only very unthinking children.
It no more occurs to us that God is engaged in
any particular work in the world than it occurs
to a little child that its father does anything except
be its father. Its father may be a Cabinet Minister
absorbed in the nation's work, or an inventor deep
in schemes for the world's good ; but to this master-
egoist he is father, and nothing more. Childhood,
whether in the physical or moral world, is the great
self-centred period of life ; and a personal God
who satisfies personal ends is all that for a long time
many a Christian understands.

But as clearly as there comes to the growing
child a knowledge of its father's part in the world,
and a sense of what real life means, there must
come to every Christian whose growth is true some

richer sense of the meaning of Christianity and a larger view of Christ's purpose for mankind. To miss this is to miss the whole splendour and glory of Christ's religion. Next to losing the sense of a personal Christ, the worst evil that can befall a Christian is to have no sense of anything else To grow up in complacent belief that God has no business in this great groaning world of human beings except to attend to a few saved souls is the negation of all religion. The first great epoch in a Christian's life, after the awe and wonder of its dawn, is when there breaks into his mind some sense that Christ has a purpose for mankind, a purpose beyond him and his needs, beyond the churches and their creeds, beyond Heaven and its saints—a purpose which embraces every man and woman born, every kindred and nation formed, which regards not their spiritual good alone but their welfare in every part, their progress, their health, their work, their wages, their happiness in this present world.

What, then, does Christ do all day ? By what further conception shall we augment the selfish view of why Christ lived and died ?

I shall mislead no one, I hope, if I say—for I wish to put the social side of Christianity in its strongest light—that Christ did not come into the

world to give men religion. He never mentioned
the word religion. Religion was in the world before
Christ came, and it lives to-day in a million souls
who have never heard His name. *What God does all
day* is not to sit waiting in churches for people to
come and worship Him. It is true that God is in
churches and in all kinds of churches, and is found
by many in churches more immediately than
anywhere else. It is also true that while Christ
did not give men religion He gave a new direction to
the religious aspiration bursting forth then and
now and always from the whole world's heart.
But it was His purpose to enlist these aspirations
on behalf of some definite practical good. The
religious people of those days did nothing with
their religion except attend to its observances.
Even the priest, after he been to the temple, thought
his work was done ; when he met the wounded
man he passed by on the other side. Christ reversed
all this—tried to reverse it, for He is only now
beginning to succeed. The tendency of the religions
of all time has been to care more for religion than
for humanity ; Christ cared more for humanity
than for religion—rather His care for humanity
was the chief expression of His religion. He was
not indifferent to observances, but the practices of
the people bulked in His thoughts before the

practices of the Church. It has been pointed out as a blemish on the immortal allegory of Bunyan that the Pilgrim never *did* anything, anything but save his soul. The remark is scarcely fair, for the allegory is designedly the story of a soul in a single relation; and, besides, he did do a little. But the warning may well be weighed. The Pilgrim's one thought, his work by day, his dream by night, was *escape*. He took little part in the world through which he passed. He was a *Pilgrim* travelling through it ; his business was to get through safe. Whatever this is, it is not Christianity. Christ's conception of Christianity was heavens removed from that of a man setting out from the City of Destruction to save his soul. It was rather that of a man dwelling amidst the Destructions of the City and planning escapes for the souls of others—escapes not to the other world, but to purity and peace and righteousness in this. In reality Christ never said " Save your soul." It is a mistranslation which says that. What He said was, " Save your life." And this not because the first is nothing, but only because it is so very great a thing that only the second can accomplish it. But the new word altruism—the translation of " love thy neighbour as thyself "— is slowly finding its way into current Christian speech. The People's Progress, not less than the

Pilgrim's Progress, is daily becoming a graver concern to the Church. A popular theology with unselfishness as part at least of its root, a theology which appeals no longer to fear, but to the generous heart in man, has already dawned, and more clearly than ever men are beginning to see what Christ really came into this world to do.

What Christ came here for was to make a better world. The world in which we live is an unfinished world. It is not wise, it is not happy, it is not pure, it is not good—it is not even sanitary. Humanity is little more than raw material. Almost everything has yet to be done to it. Before the days of Geology people thought the earth was finished. It is by no means finished. The work of Creation is going on. Before the spectroscope, men thought the universe was finished. We know now it is just beginning. And this teeming universe of men in which we live has almost all its finer colour and beauty yet to take. Christ came to complete it. The fires of its passions were not yet cool ; their heat had to be transformed into finer energies. The ideals for its future were all to shape, the forces to realise them were not yet born. The poison of its sins had met no antidote, the gloom of its doubt no light, the weight of its sorrow no rest. These the Saviour of the world, the Light of men, would do and be. This, roughly, was His scheme.

Now this was a prodigious task—to recreate the world. How was it to be done ? God's way of making worlds is to make them make themselves. When He made the earth He made a rough ball of matter and supplied it with a multitude of tools to mould it into form—the rain-drop to carve it, the glacier to smooth it, the river to nourish it, the flower to adorn it. God works always with agents, and this is our way when we want any great thing done, and this was Christ's way when He undertook the finishing of Humanity. He had a vast intractable mass of matter to deal with, and He required a multitude of tools. Christ's tools were men. Hence His first business in the world was to make a collection of men. In other words He founded a Society.

THE FOUNDING OF THE SOCIETY

It is a somewhat startling thought—it will not be misunderstood—that Christ probably did not save many people while He was here. Many an evangelist in that direction has done much more. He never intended to finish the world single-handed, but announced from the first that others would not only take part, but do " greater things " than He. For amazing as was the attention He was able to give to individuals, this was not the whole aim He had in view. His immediate work was to enlist men in His enterprise, to rally them into a great company or Society for the carrying out of His plans.

The name by which this Society was known was *The Kingdom of God*. Christ did not coin this name ; it was an old expression, and good men had always hoped and prayed that some such Society would be born in their midst. But it was never either defined or set agoing in earnest until Christ made its realisation the passion of His life.

How keenly He felt regarding His task, how enthusiastically He set about it, every page of His life bears witness. All reformers have one or two great words which they use incessantly, and by mere reiteration imbed indelibly in the thought and history of their time. Christ's great word was the Kingdom of God. Of all the words of His that have come down to us this is by far the commonest. One hundred times it occurs in the Gospels. When He preached He had almost always this for a text. His sermons were explanations of the aims of His Society, of the different things it was like, of

whom its membership consisted, what they were
to do or to be, or not do or not be. And even when
He does not actually use the word, it is easy to
see that all He said and did had reference to this.
Philosophers talk about thinking in categories—
the mind living, as it were, in a particular room
with its own special furniture, pictures, and view-
points, these giving a consistent direction and colour
to all that is there thought or expressed. It was in
the category of the Kingdom that Christ's thought
moved. Though one time He said He came to
save the lost, or at another time to give men life,
or to do His Father's will, these were all included
among the objects of His Society.

No one can ever know what Christianity is till
he has grasped this leading thought in the mind of
Christ. Peter and Paul have many wonderful and
necessary things to tell us about what Christ was
and did ; but we are looking now at what Cdrist's
own thought was. Do not think this is a mere
modern theory. These are His own life-plans taken
from His own lips. Do not allow any isolated text,
even though it seem to sum up for you the Christian
life, to keep you from trying to understand Christ's
Programme as a whole. The perspective of Christ's
teaching is not everything, but without it everything will be distorted and untrue. There is much

good in a verse, but often much evil. To see some small soul pirouetting throughout life on a single text, and judging all the world because it cannot find a partner, is not a Christian sight. Christianity does not grudge such souls their comfort. What it grudges is that they make Christ's Kingdom uninhabitable to thoughtful minds. Be sure that whenever the religion of Christ appears small, or forbidding, or narrow, or inhuman, you are dealing not with the whole—which is a matchless moral symmetry—nor even with an arch or column—for every detail is perfect—but with some cold stone removed from its place and suggesting nothing of the glorious structure from which it came.

Tens of thousands of persons who are familiar with religious truths have not noticed yet that Christ ever founded a Society at all. The reason is partly that people have read texts instead of reading their Bible, partly that they have studied Theology instead of studying Christianity, and partly because of the noiselessness and invisibility of the Kingdom of God itself. Nothing truer was ever said of this Kingdom than that " It cometh without observation." Its first discovery, therefore, comes to the Christian with all the force of a revelation. The sense of belonging to such a Society transforms life. It is the difference between being a solitary knight tilting single-handed, and often defeated, at whatever enemy one chances to meet on one's little acre of life, and the *feel* of belonging to a mighty army marching throughout all time to a certain victory. This note of universality given to even the humblest work we do, this sense of comradeship, this link with history, this thought of a definite campaign, this promise of success, is the possession of every obscurest unit in the Kingdom of God.

THE PROGRAMME OF THE SOCIETY

HUNDREDS of years before Christ's Society was formed, its Programme had been issued to the world. I cannot think of any scene in history more dramatic than when Jesus entered the church in Nazareth and read it to the people. Not that when He appropriated to Himself that venerable fragment from Isaiah He was uttering a manifesto or announcing His formal Programme. Christ never did things formally. We think of the words, as He probably thought of them, not in their old-world historical significance, nor as a full expression of His future aims, but as a summary of great moral facts now and always to be realised in the world since he appeared.

Remember as you read the words to what grim reality they refer. Recall what Christ's problem really was, what His Society was founded for. This Programme deals with a real world. Think of it as you read—not of the surface-world, but of the world as it is, as it sins and weeps, and curses and suffers and sends up its long cry to God. Limit it if you like to the world around your door, but think of it—of the city and the hospital and the dungeon and the graveyard, of the sweating-shop and the pawn-shop and the drink-shop; think of the cold, the cruelty, the fever, the famine, the ugliness, the loneliness, the pain. And then try to keep down the lump in your throat as you take up His Programme and read—

To Bind up the Broken-Hearted :
To Proclaim Liberty to the Captives :
To Comfort all that Mourn :
To Give unto them—
> Beauty for Ashes,
> The Oil of Joy for Mourning,
> The Garment of Praise for the Spirit of Heaviness.

What an exchange—Beauty for Ashes, Joy for Mourning, Liberty for Chains! No marvel " the eyes of all them that were in the synagogue were fastened on Him " as He read ; or that they " wondered at the gracious words which proceeded out of His lips." Only one man in that congregation, only one man in the world to-day could hear these accents with dismay—the man, the culprit, who has said hard words of Christ.

We are all familiar with the protest, " Of course " —as if there were no other alternative to a person of culture—" Of course I am not a Christian, but I always speak *respectfully* of Christianity." Respectfully of Christianity ! No remark fills one's soul with such sadness. One can understand a man as he reads these words being stricken speechless ; one can see the soul within him rise to a white heat as each fresh benediction falls upon his ear and drives him, a half-mad enthusiast, to bear them to the world. But in what school has he learned of Christ who offers the Saviour of the world his respect ?

Men repudiate Christ's religion because they think it a small and limited thing, a scheme with no large human interests to commend it to this great social age. I ask you to note that there is not one burning interest of the human race which is not represented here. What are the great words of Christianity according to this Programme ! Take as specimens these :

> LIBERTY,
>
> COMFORT,
>
> BEAUTY,
>
> JOY.

These are among the greatest words of life. Give them their due extension, the significance which Christ undoubtedly saw in them and which Christianity undoubtedly yields, and there is almost no great want or interest of mankind which they do not cover.

These are not only the greatest words of life, but they are the best. This Programme, to those who have misread Christianity, is a series of surprises. Observe the most prominent note in it. It is *gladness*. Its first word is " good-tidings," its last is " joy." The saddest words of life are also there—but there as the diseases which Christianity comes to cure. No life that is occupied with such an enterprise could be other than radiant. The contribution of Christianity to the joy of the living, perhaps even more to the joy of *thinking*, is unspeakable. The joyful life is the life of the larger mission, the disinterested life, the life of the overflow from self, the " more abundant life " which comes from following Christ. And the joy of thinking is the larger thinking, the thinking of the man who holds in his hand some Programme for Humanity. The Christian is the only man who has any Programme at all—any Programme either for the world or for himself. Goethe, Byron, Carlyle taught Humanity much, but they had no Programme for it. Byron's thinking was suffering; Carlyle's despair. Christianity alone exults. The belief in the universe as moral, the interpretation of history as progress, the faith in good as eternal, in evil as self-consuming, in humanity as evolving— these Christian ideas have transformed the malady of thought into a bounding hope. It was no sentiment but a conviction matured amid calamity and submitted to the tests of life that inspired the great modern poet of optimism to proclaim:

" Gladness be with thee, Helper of the world !
  I think this is the authentic sign and seal
  Of Godship, that ever waxes glad,
  And more glad, until gladness blossoms, bursts
  Into a rage to suffer for mankind
  And recommence at sorrow."

But that is not all. Man's greatest needs are often very homely. And it is almost as much in its fearless recognition of the commonplace woes of life, and its deliberate offerings to minor needs, that the claims of Christianity to be a religion for Humanity stand. Look, for instance, at the closing sentence of this Programme. Who would have expected to find among the special objects of Christ's solicitude the *Spirit of Heaviness* ? Supreme needs, many and varied, had been already dealt with on this Programme ; many applicants had been met ; the list is about to close. Suddenly the writer remembers the nameless malady of the poor—that mysterious disease which the rich share but cannot alleviate, which is too subtle for doctors, too incurable for Parliaments, too unpicturesque for philanthropy. too common even for sympathy. Can Christ meet that ?

If Christianity could even deal with the world's Depression, could cure mere dull spirits, it would be the Physician of Humanity. But it can. It has the secret, a hundred secrets, for the lifting of the world's gloom. It cannot immediately remove the physiological causes of dulness—though obedience to its principles can do an infinity to prevent them, and its inspirations can do even more to lift the mind above them. But where the causes are moral or mental or social, the remedy is in every Christian's hand. Think of any one at this moment whom the

Spirit of Heaviness haunts. You think of a certain old woman But you know for a fact that you can cure her. You did so, perfectly, only a week ago. A mere visit, and a little present, or the visit without any present, set her up for seven long days, and seven long nights. The machinery of the Kingdom is very simple and very silent, and the most silent parts do most, and we all believe so little in the medicines of Christ that we do not know what ripples of healing are set in motion when we simply smile on one another. Christianity wants nothing so much in the world as sunny people, and the old are hungrier for love than for bread, and the Oil of Joy is very cheap, and if you can help the poor on with a Garment of Praise, it will be better for them than blankets.

Or perhaps you know someone else who is dull—not an old woman this time but a very rich and important man. But you also know perfectly what makes him dull. It is either his riches or his importance. Christianity can cure either of these —though you may not be the person to apply the cure—at a single hearing. Or here is a third case, one of your own servants. It is a case of *monotony*. Prescribe more variety, leisure, recreation- anything to relieve the wearing strain. A fourth case – your most honoured guest: Condition—leisure, health, accomplishments, means; Disease—Spiritual Obesity; Treatment—talent to be put out to usury. And so on down the whole range of life's dejection and *ennui*

Perhaps you tell me this is not Christianity at all; that everybody could do that. The curious thing is that everybody does not. Good-will to men came into the world with Christ, and wherever that is found, in Christian or heathen land, there Christ is, and there His spirit works. And if you say that the chief end of Christianity is not the world's happiness, I agree; it was never meant to be; but the strange fact is that, without making it its chief end, it wholly and infallibly, and quite universally, leads to it. Hence the note of Joy, though not the highest on Christ's Programme, is a loud and ringing note, and none who serve in His Society can be long without its music. Time was when a Christian used to apologise for being happy. But the day has always been when he ought to apologise for being miserable.

Christianity, you will observe, really works. And it succeeds not only because it is divine, but because it is so very human—because it is common-sense. Why should the Garment of Praise destroy the Spirit of Heaviness? Because an old woman cannot sing and cry at the same moment. The

Society of Christ is a sane Society. Its methods are rational. The principle in the old woman's case is simply that one emotion destroys another. Christianity works, as a railway man would say, with points. It switches souls from valley lines to mountain lines, not stemming the currents of life but diverting them. In the rich man's case the principle of cure is different, but it is again principle, not necromancy. His spirit of heaviness is caused, like any other heaviness, by the earth's attraction. Take away the earth and you take away the attraction. But if Christianity can do anything it can take away the earth. By the wider extension of the horizon which it gives, by the new standard of values, by the mere setting of life's small pomps and interests and admirations in the light of the Eternal, it dissipates the world with a breath. All that tends to abolish worldliness tends to abolish unrest, and hence, in the rush of modern life, one far-reaching good of all even commonplace Christian preaching, all Christian literature, all which holds the world doggedly to the idea of a God and a future life, and reminds mankind of Infinity and Eternity.

Side by side with these influences, yet taking the world at a wholly different angle, works another great Christian force. How many opponents of religion are aware that one of the specific objects of Christ's Society is Beauty ? The charge of vulgarity against Christianity is an old one. If it means that Christianity deals with the ruder elements in human nature, it is true, and that is its glory. But if it means that it has no respect for the finer qualities, the charge is baseless. For Christianity not only encourages whatsoever things are lovely, but wars against that whole theory of life which would exclude them. It prescribes æstheticism. It proscribes asceticism And for those who preach to Christians that in these enlightened days they must raise the masses by giving them noble sculptures and beautiful paintings and music and public parks, the answer is that these things are all already being given, and given daily, and with an increasing sense of their importance, by the Society of Christ. Take away from the world the beautiful things which have not come from Christ and you will make it poorer scarcely at all. Take away from modern cities the paintings, the monuments, the music for the people, the museums and the parks which are not the gifts of Christian men and Christian municipalities, and in ninety cases out of a hundred you will leave them unbereft of so much as a well-shaped lamp-post.

It is impossible to doubt that the Decorator of

the World shall not continue to serve to His later children, and in ever finer forms, the inspirations of beautiful things. More fearlessly than he has ever done, the Christian of modern life will use the noble spiritual leverages of Art. That this world, the people's world, is a bleak and ugly world, we do not forget ; it is ever with us. But we esteem too little the mission of beautiful things in haunting the mind with higher thoughts and begetting the mood which leads to God. Physical beauty makes moral beauty. Loveliness does more than destroy ugliness ; it destroys matter. A mere touch of it in a room, in a street, even on a door knocker, is a spiritual force. Ask the working-man's wife, and she will tell you there is a moral effect even in a clean table-cloth. If a barrel-organ in a slum can but drown a curse, let no Christian silence it. The mere light and colour of the wall-advertisements are a gift of God to the poor man's sombre world.

One Christmas-time a poor drunkard told me that he had gone out the night before to take his usual chance of the temptations of the street. Close to his door, at a shop window, an angel—so he said—arrested him. It was a large Christmas-card, a glorious white thing with tinsel wings, and as it glittered in the gas-light it flashed into his soul a sudden thought of Heaven. It recalled the earlier heaven of his infancy, and he thought of his mother in the distant glen, and how it would please her if she got this Christmas angel from her prodigal. With money already pledged to the devil he bought the angel, and with it a new soul and future for himself. That was a real angel. For that day as I saw its tinsel pinions shine in his squalid room I knew what Christ's angels were. They are all beautiful things, which daily in common homes are bearing up heavy souls to God.

But do not misunderstand me. This angel was made of pasteboard: a pasteboard angel can never save a soul. Tinsel reflects the sun, but warms nothing. Our Programme must go deeper. Beauty may arrest the drunkard, but it cannot cure him.

It is here that Christianity asserts itself with a supreme individuality. It is here that it parts company with Civilisation, with Politics, with all secular schemes of Social Reform. In its diagnosis of human nature it finds that which most other systems ignore ; which, if they see, they cannot cure ; which, left undestroyed, makes every reform futile, and every inspiration vain. That thing is *Sin*. Christianity, of all other philanthropies, recognises that man's devouring need is *Liberty*— liberty to stop sinning ; to leave the prison of his

passions, and shake off the fetters of his past.
To surround *Captives* with statues and pictures,
to offer *Them-that-are-Bound* a higher wage or a
cleaner street or a few more cubic feet of air per
head, is solemn trifling It is a cleaner soul they
want ; a purer air, or any air at all, for their higher
selves.

And where the cleaner soul is to come from
apart from Christ I cannot tell. " By no political
alchemy," Herbert Spencer tells us, " can you get
golden conduct out of leaden instincts." The power
to set the heart right, to renew the springs of action,
comes from Christ. The sense of the infinite worth
of the single soul, and the recoverableness of man
at his worst, are the gifts of Christ. The freedom
from guilt, the forgiveness of sins, come from Christ's
Cross ; the hope of immortality springs from
Christ's grave. We believe in the gospel of better
laws and an improved environment ; we hold the
religion of Christ to be a social religion ; we magnify
and call Christian the work of reformers, statesmen,
philanthropists, educators, inventors, sanitary
officers, and all who directly or remotely aid, abet,
or further the higher progress of mankind ; but in
Him alone, in the fulness of that word, do we see
the Saviour of the world.

There are earnest and gifted lives to-day at work

among the poor whose lips at least will not name the name of Christ. I speak of them with respect ; their shoe-latchets many of us are not worthy to unloose. But because the creed of the neighbouring mission-hall is a travesty of religion they refuse to acknowledge the power of the living Christ to stop man's sin, of the dying Christ to forgive it. O, narrowness of breadth ! Because there are ignorant doctors do I yet rail at medicine or start an hospital of my own ? Because the poor raw evangelist, or the narrow ecclesiastic, offer their little all to the poor, shall I repudiate all they do not know of Christ because of the little that they do know ? Of gospels for the poor which have not some theory, state it how you will, of personal conversion one cannot have much hope. Personal conversion means for life a personal religion, a personal trust in God, a personal debt to Christ, a personal dedication to His cause. These, brought about how you will, are supreme things to aim at, supreme losses if they are missed. Sanctification will come to masses only as it comes to individual men ; and to work with Christ's Programme and ignore Christ is to utilise the sun's light without its energy.

But this is not the only point at which the uniqueness of this Society appears. There is yet another depth in humanity which no other system

even attempts to sound. We live in a world not
only of sin but of sorrow—

"There is no flock, however watched and tended,
   But one dead lamb is there ;
There is no home, howe'er defended,
   But has one vacant chair."

When the flock thins, and the chair empties, who
is to be near to heal ? At that moment the gospels
of the world are on trial. In the presence of death
how will they act ? Act ! They are blotted out
of existence. Philosophy, Politics, Reforms, are
no more. The Picture Galleries close. The Sculptures hide. The Committees disperse. There is
crape on the door ; the world withdraws. Observe,
it withdraws. It has no mission.

So awful in its loneliness was this hour that the
Romans paid a professional class to step in with
its mummeries and try to fill it. But that is Christ's
own hour. Next to Righteousness the greatest word
of Christianity is Comfort. Christianity has almost
a monopoly of Comfort. Renan was never nearer
the mark than when he spoke of the Bible as " the
great Book of the Consolation of Humanity."
Christ's Programme is full of Comfort, studded with
Comfort : " to bind up the Broken-Hearted, to

Comfort all that mourn, to Give unto them that mourn in Zion." Even the " good tidings " to the " meek " are, in the Hebrew, a message to the " afflicted " or " the poor." The word Gospel itself comes down through the Greek from this very passage, so that whatever else Christ's Gospel means it is first an Evangel for suffering men.

One note in this Programme jars with all the rest. When Christ read from Isaiah that day He never finished the passage. A terrible word, Vengeance, yawned like a precipice across His path ; and in the middle of a sentence " He closed the Book, and gave it again to the minister, and sat down." A Day of Vengeance from our God— these were the words before which Christ paused. When the prophet proclaimed it some great historical fulfilment was in his mind. Had the people to whom Christ read been able to understand its ethical equivalents He would probably have read on. For, so understood, instead of filling the mind with fear, the thought of this Dread Day inspires it with a solemn gratitude. The work of the Avenger is a necessity. It is part of God's philanthropy.

For I have but touched the surface in speaking of the sorrow of the world as if it came from people dying. It comes from people living. Before ever the Broken-Hearted can be healed a hundred greater causes of suffering than death must be destroyed. Before the Captive can be free a vaster prison than his own sins must be demolished. There are hells on earth into which no breath of heaven can ever come ; these must be swept away. There are social soils in which only unrighteousness can flourish ; these must be broken up.

And that is the work of the Day of Vengeance. When is that day ? It is now Who is the Avenger ? Law. What Law ? Criminal Law, Sanitary Law, Social Law, Natural Law. Wherever the poor are trodden upon or tread upon one another ; wherever the air is poison and the water foul ; wherever want stares, and vice reigns, and rags rot—there the Avenger takes his stand. Whatever makes it more difficult for the drunkard to reform, for the children to be pure, for the widow to earn a wage, for any of the wheels of progress to revolve—with these he deals. Delay him not. He is the messenger of Christ. Despair of him not, distrust him not His Day dawns slowly, but his work is sure. Though evil stalks the world, it is on the way to execution ; though wrong reigns, it must end in self-combustion. The very nature of things is God's Avenger ; the very story of civilisation is the history of Christ's Throne.

Anything that prepares the way for a better social state is the fit work of the followers of Christ. Those who work on the more spiritual levels leave too much unhonoured the slow toil of multitudes of unchurched souls who prepare the material or moral environments without which these higher labours are in vain. Prevention is Christian as well as cure ; and Christianity travels sometimes by the most circuitous paths It is given to some to work for immediate results, and from year to year they are privileged to reckon up a balance of success. But these are not always the greatest in the Kingdom of God. The men who get no stimulus from any visible reward, whose lives pass while the objects for which they toil are still too far away to comfort them ; the men who hold aloof from dazzling schemes and earn the misunderstanding of the crowd because they foresee remoter issues, who even oppose a seeming good because a deeper evil lurks beyond—these are the *statesmen* of the Kingdom of God.

THE MACHINERY OF THE SOCIETY

Such in dimmest outline is the Programme of Christ's Society. Did you know that all this was going on in the world ? Did you know that Christianity was such a living and purpose-like thing ? Look back to the day when that Programme was given, and you will see that it was not merely written on paper. Watch the drama of the moral order rise up, scene after scene, in history. Study the social evolution of humanity, the spread of righteousness, the amelioration of life, the freeing of slaves, the elevation of woman, the purification of religion, and ask what these can be if not the coming of the Kingdom of God on earth. For it is precisely through the movements of nations and the lives of men that this Kingdom comes. Christ might have done all this work Himself, with His own hands. But He did not. The crowning wonder of His scheme is that he entrusted it to *men.* It is the supreme glory of humanity that the machinery for its redemption should have been placed within itself. I think the saddest thing in Christ's life was that after founding a Society with aims so glorious He had to go away and leave it.

But in reality He did not leave it. The old theory

that God made the world, made it as an inventor would make a machine, and then stood looking on to see it work, has passed away. God is no longer a remote spectator of the natural world, but immanent in it, pervading matter by His present Spirit, and ordering it by His Will. So Christ is immanent in men. His work is to move the hearts and inspire the lives of men, and through such hearts to move and reach the world. Men, only men, can carry out this work. This humanness, this inwardness, of the Kingdom is one reason why some scarcely see that it exists at all. We measure great movement by the loudness of their advertisement, or the place their externals fill in the public eye. This Kingdom has no externals. The usual methods of propagating a great cause were entirely discarded by Christ. The sword He declined; money He had none; literature He never used; the Church disowned Him; the State crucified Him. Planting His ideals in the hearts of a few poor men, He started them out unheralded to revolutionise the world. They did it by making friends—and by making enemies; they went about, did good, sowed seed, died, and lived again in the lives of those they helped. These in turn, a fraction of them, did the same. They met, they prayed, they talked of Christ, they loved, they went among other men, and by act and word passed on their secret. The machinery of the Kingdom of God is purely social. It acts, not by commandment, but by contagion ; not by fiat, but by friendship. " The Kingdom of God is like unto leaven, which a woman took and hid in three measures of meal till the whole was leavened."

After all, like all great discoveries once they are made, this seems absolutely the most feasible method that could have been devised. Men *must* live among men. Men *must* influence men. Organisations, institutions, churches, have too much rigidity for a thing that is to flood the world. The only fluid in the world is man. War might have won for Christ's cause a passing victory ; wealth might have purchased a superficial triumph ; political power might have gained a temporary success. But in these there is no note of universality, of solidarity, of immortality. To live through the centuries and pervade the uttermost ends of the earth, to stand while kingdoms tottered and civilisations changed, to survive fallen churches and crumbling creeds there was no soil for the Kingdom of God like the hearts of common men. Some who have written about this Kingdom have emphasised its moral grandeur, others its universality, others its adaptation to man's needs. One great writer speaks of its prodigious originality, another chiefly notices its success. I confess what almost strikes me most is the miracle of its simplicity.

Men, then, are the only means God's Spirit has of accomplishing His purpose. What men ? You. Is it worth doing, or is it not ? Is it worth while joining Christ's Society or is it not ? What do *you* do all day ? What is your personal stake in the coming of the Kingdom of Christ on earth ? You are not interested in religion, you tell me ; you do not care for your " soul." It was not about your religion I ventured to ask, still less about your soul. That you have no religion, that you do not care for your soul, does not absolve you from caring for the world in which you live. But you do not believe in this church, you reply, or accept this doctrine, or that. Christ does not, in the first instance, ask your thoughts, but your work. No man has a right to postpone his *life* for the sake of his thoughts. Why ? Because this is a real world, not a *think* world. Treat it as a real world—act. Think by all means, but think also of what is actual, of what like the stern world is, of how much even you, creedless and churchless, could do to make it better. The thing to be anxious about is not to be right with man, but with mankind. And, so far as I know, there is nothing so on all fours with mankind as Christianity.

There are versions of Christianity, it is true, which no self-respecting mind can do other than disown—versions so hard, so narrow, so unreal, so super-theological, that practical men can find in them neither outlet for their lives nor resting-place for their thoughts. With these we have nothing to do. With these Christ had nothing to do—except to oppose them with every word and act of His life. It too seldom occurs to those who repudiate Christianity because of its narrowness or its unpracticalness, its sanctimoniousness or its dulness, that these were the very things which Christ strove against and unweariedly condemned. It was the one risk of His religion being given to the common people—an inevitable risk which He took without reserve—that its infinite lustre should be tarnished in the fingering of the crowd or have its great truths narrowed into mean and unworthy moulds as they passed from lip to lip. But though the crowd is the object of Christianity, it is not its custodian. Deal with the Founder of this great Commonwealth Himself. Any man of honest purpose who will take the trouble to inquire at first hand what Christianity really is, will find it a thing he cannot get away from. Without either argument or pressure by the mere practicalness of its aims and the pathos of its compassions, it forces its august claim upon every serious life.

He who joins this Society finds himself in a large place. The Kingdom of God is a Society of the best men, working for the best ends, according to the best methods. Its membership is a multitude whom no man can number ; its methods are as various as human nature ; its field is the world. It is a Commonwealth, yet it honours a King ; it is a Social Brotherhood, but it acknowledges the Fatherhood of God. Though not a Philosophy the world turns to it for light ; though not Political it is the incubator of all great laws. It is more human than the State, for it deals with deeper needs ; more Catholic than the Church, for it includes whom the Church rejects. It is a Propaganda, yet it works not by agitation but by ideals. It is a Religion, yet it holds the worship of God to be mainly the service of man. Though not a Scientific Society its watchword is Evolution ; though not an Ethic it possesses the Sermon on the Mount. This mysterious Society owns no wealth but distributes fortunes. It has no minutes for history keeps them ; no member's roll for no one could make it. Its entry-money is nothing ; its subscription, all you have. The Society never

meets and it never adjourns. Its law is one word
—loyalty ; its Gospel one message—love. Verily
" Whosoever will lose his life for My sake shall find
it."

The Programme for the other life is not out yet.
For this world, for these faculties, for his one short
life, I know nothing that is offered to man to compare with membership in the Kingdom of God.
Among the mysteries which compass the world
beyond, none is greater than how there can be in
store for man a work more wonderful, a life more
God-like than this. If you know anything better,
live for it ; if not, in the name of God and of
Humanity, carry out Christ's plan.

III.

THE
CITY WITHOUT A CHURCH

I, John,
Saw the Holy City,
New Jerusalem,
Coming down from God out of Heaven.

And I saw no Temple therein.

And His servants shall serve Him.
And they shall see His Face
And His Name shall be written on their foreheads.

THE
CITY WITHOUT A CHURCH

I SAW THE CITY

Two very startling things arrest us in John's vision of the future. The first is that the likest thing to Heaven he could think of was a City ; the second, that there was no Church in that City.

Almost nothing more revolutionary could be said, even to the modern world, in the name of religion. *No Church*—that is the defiance of religion ; a *City*—that is the antipodes of Heaven. Yet John combines these contradictions in one daring image, and holds up to the world the picture of a City without a Chnrch as his ideal of the heavenly life.

By far the most original thing here is the simple conception of Heaven as a City. The idea of religion without a Church—" I saw no Temple therein "— is anomalous enough ; but the association of the blessed life with a City—the one place in the world from which Heaven seems most far away—is something wholly new in religious thought. No other religion which has a Heaven ever had a Heaven like this. The Greek, if he looked forward at all, awaited the Elysian Fields ; the Eastern sought Nirvana. All other Heavens have been Gardens, Dreamlands—passivities more or less aimless. Even to the majority among ourselves Heaven is a siesta and not a City It remained for John to go straight to the other extreme and select the citadel of the world's fever, the ganglion of its unrest, the heart and focus of its most strenuous toil, as the frame-work for his ideal of the blessed life.

The Heaven of Christianity is different from all other Heavens, because the religion of Christianity is different from all other religions. Christianity is the religion of Cities. It moves among real things. Its sphere is the street, the market-place, the working-life of the world.

And what interests one for the present in John's vision is not so much what it reveals of a Heaven beyond, but what it suggests of the nature of the heavenly life in this present world. Find out what a man's Heaven is—no matter whether it be a dream or a reality, no matter whether it refer to an actual Heaven or to a Kingdom of God to be realised on earth—and you pass by an easy discovery to what his religion is. And herein lies one value at least of this allegory. It is a touch-stone for Christianity, a test for the solidity or the insipidity of one's religion, for the wholesomeness or the fatuousness of one's faith, for the usefulness or the futility of one's life. For this vision of the City marks off in lines which no eye can mistake the true area which the religion of Christ is meant to inhabit, and announces for all time the real nature of the saintly life

City life is human life at its intensest, man in his most real relations. And the nearer one draws to reality, the nearer one draws to the working sphere of religion Wherever real life is, there Christ goes. And He goes there, not only because the great need lies there, but because there is found, so to speak, the raw material with which Christianity works—the life of man. To do something with this, to infuse something into this, to save and inspire and sanctify this, the actual working life of the world, is what He came for Without human life to act upon, without the relations of men with one another, of master with servant, husband with wife, buyer with seller, creditor with debtor, there is no such thing as Christianity With actual things, with Humanity in its everyday dress, with the traffic of the streets, with gates and houses, with work and wages, with sin and poverty, with these *things*, and all the things and all the relations and all the people of the City, Christianity has to do, and has more to do than with anything else. To conceive of the Christian religion as itself a thing—a something which can exist apart from life ; to think of it as something added on to being, something kept in a separate compartment called the soul, as an extra accomplishment like music, or a special talent like art, is totally to misapprehend its nature. It is that which fills all compartments. It is that which makes the whole life music and every separate action a work of art Take away action and it is not Take away people, houses, streets, character, and it ceases to be Without these there may be sentiment, or rapture, or adoration, or superstition ; there may even be religion, but there can never be the religion of the Son of Man.

If Heaven were a siesta, religion might be conceived of as a reverie. If the future life were to be mainly spent in a Temple, the present life might be mainly spent in Church But if Heaven be a City, the life of those who are going there must be a real life The man who would enter John's Heaven, no matter what piety or what faith he may profess, must be a real man. Christ's gift to men was life, a rich and abundant life And life is meant for living An abundant life does not show itself in abundant dreaming, but in abundant living —in abundant living among real and tangible objects and to actual and practical purposes. "His servants," John tells us, "shall serve." In this vision of the City he confronts us with a new definition of a Christian man—the perfect saint is the perfect citizen.

To make Cities—that is what we are here for. To make good Cities—that is for the present hour the main work of Christianity. For the City is strategic. It makes the towns : the towns make the villages ; the villages make the country. He who makes the City makes the world. After all, though men make Cities, it is Cities which make men. Whether our national life is great or mean, whether our social virtues are mature or stunted, whether our sons are moral or vicious, whether religion is possible or impossible, depends upon the City. When Christianity shall take upon itself in full responsibility the burden and care of Cities the Kingdom of God will openly come on earth. What Christianity waits for also, as its final apologetic and justification to the world, is the founding of a City which shall be in visible reality a City of God. People do not dispute that religion is in the Church. What is now wanted is to let them see it in the City.

One Christian City, one City in any part of the earth, whose citizens from the greatest to the humblest lived in the spirit of Christ, where religion had over-flowed the Churches and passed into the streets, inundating every house and workshop, and per-meating the whole social and commercial life—one such Christian City would seal the redemption of the world.

Some such City, surely, was what John saw in his dream. Whatever reference we may find there to a world to come, is it not equally lawful to seek the scene upon this present world? John saw his City *descending out of Heaven*. It was, moreover, no strange apparition, but a City which he knew. It was Jerusalem, a new *Jerusalem*. The significance of that name has been altered for most of us by religious poetry; we spell it with a capital and speak of the New Jerusalem as a synonym for Heaven. Yet why not take it simply as it stands, as a new Jerusalem? Try to restore the natural force of the expression—suppose John to have lived to-day and to have said London? "I saw a new London?" Jerusalem was John's London. All the grave and sad suggestion that the word London brings up to-day to the modern reformer, the word Jerusalem recalled to him. What in his deepest hours he longed and prayed for was a new Jerusalem,

a reformed Jerusalem. And just as it is given
to the man in modern England who is a prophet,
to the man who believes in God and in the moral
order of the world, to discern a new London shaping
itself through all the sin and chaos of the City,
so was it given to John to see a new Jerusalem
rise from the ruins of the old.

We have no concern—it were contrary to critical
method—to press the allegory in detail. What we
take from it, looked at in this light, is the broad
conception of a transformed City, the great Christian
thought that the very Cities where we live, with
all their suffering and sin, shall one day, by the
gradual action of the forces of Christianity, be
turned into Heavens on earth. This is a spectacle
which profoundly concerns the world. To the
reformer, the philanthropist, the economist, the
politician, this Vision of the City is the great classic
of social literature. What John saw, we may fairly
take it, was the future of all Cities. It was the dawn
of a new social order, a regenerate humanity, a
purified society, an actual transformation of the
Cities of the world into Cities of God.

This City, then, which John saw is none other
than your City, the place where you live—as it
might be, and as you are to help to make it. It is
London, Berlin, New York, Paris, Melbourne,

Calcutta—these as they might be, and in some infinitesimal degree as they have already begun to be. In each of these, and in every City throughout the world to-day, there is a City descending out of Heaven from God. Each one of us is daily building up this City or helping to keep it back. Its walls rise slowly, but, as we believe in God, the building can never cease. For the might of those who build, be they few or many, is so surely greater than the might of those who retard, that no day's sun sets over any City in the land that does not see some stone of the invisible City laid. To believe this is faith. To live for this is Christianity.

The project is delirious? Yes—to atheism. To John it was the most obvious thing in the world. Nay, knowing all he knew, its realisation was inevitable. We forget, when the thing strikes us as strange, that John knew Christ. Christ was the Light of the World—the Light of the *World*. This is all that he meant by his Vision, that Christ is the Light of the World. This Light, John saw, would fall everywhere—especially upon Cities. It was irresistible and inextinguishable. No darkness could stand before it. One by one the Cities of the world would give up their night. Room by room, house by house, street by street, they would be changed. Whatsoever worketh abomination or maketh a lie would disappear. Sin, pain, sorrow, would silently pass away. One day the walls of the City would be jasper ; the very streets would be paved with gold. Then the kings of the earth would bring their glory and honour into it. In the midst of the streets there should be a tree of Life. And its leaves would go forth for the healing of the nations.

Survey the Cities of the world to-day, survey your own City—town, village, home—and prophesy. God's kingdom is surely to come in this world. God's will is surely to be done on earth as it is done in Heaven. Is not this one practicable way of realising it ? When a prophet speaks of something that is to be, that coming event is usually brought about by no unrelated cause or sudden shock, but in the ordered course of the world's drama. With Christianity as the supreme actor in the world's drama, the future of its Cities is even now quite clear. Project the lines of Christian and social progress to their still far off goal, and see even now that Heaven must come to earth.

HIS SERVANTS SHALL SERVE

IF any one wishes to know what he can do to help on the work of God in the world let him make a City, or a street, or a house of a City. Men complain of the indefiniteness of religion. There are thousands ready in their humble measure to offer some personal service for the good of men, but they do not know where to begin. Let me tell you where to begin——where Christ told His disciples to begin, at the nearest City. I promise you that before one week's work is over you will never again be haunted by the problem of the indefiniteness of Christianity. You will see so much to do, so many actual things to be set right, so many merely material conditions to alter, so much striving with employers of labour, and City-councils, and trade agitators, and Boards, and Vestries, and Committees ; so much pure unrelieved uninspiring hard work, that you will begin to wonder whether in all this naked realism you are on holy ground at all. Do not be afraid of missing Heaven in seeking a better earth. The distinction between secular and sacred is a confusion and not a contrast ; and it is only because the secular is so intensely sacred that so many eyes are blind before it. The really secular thing in life is the spirit which despises under that name what is but part of the everywhere present work and will of God. Be sure that, down to the last and pettiest detail, all that concerns a better world is the direct concern of Christ.

I make this, then, in all seriousness as a definite practical proposal. You wish, you say, to be a religious man. Well, be one. There is your City; begin. But what are you to believe? Believe in your City. What else? In Jesus Christ. What about him? That He wants to make your City better; that that is what He would be doing if He lived there. What else? Believe in yourself—that you, even you, can do some of the work which He would like done, and that unless you do it, it will remain undone. How are you to begin? As Christ did. First He looked at the City; then He wept over it; then He died for it.

Where are you to begin? Begin where you are. Make that one corner, room, house, office, as like Heaven as you can. Begin? Begin with the paper on the walls, make that beautiful; with the air, keep it fresh; with the very drains, make them sweet; with the furniture, see that it be honest. Abolish whatsoever worketh abomination—in food, in drink, in luxury, in books, in art; whatsoever maketh a lie—in conversation, in social intercourse, in correspondence, in domestic life. This done, you have arranged for a Heaven, but you have not got it. Heaven lies within, in kindness, in humbleness, in unselfishness, in faith, in love, in service. to get these in, get Christ in. Teach all in the house about Christ—what He did, and what He said, and how He lived, and how He died, and how He dwells in them, and how He makes all one. Teach it not as a doctrine, but as a discovery, as your own discovery. Live your own discovery.

Then pass out into the City. Do all to it that you have done at home. Beautify it, ventilate it, drain it. Let nothing enter it that can defile the streets, the stage, the newspaper offices, the booksellers' counters; nothing that maketh a lie in its warehouses, its manufactures, its shops, its art galleries, its advertisements. Educate it, amuse it, church it. Christianise capital; dignify labour. Join Councils and Committees. Provide for the poor, the sick, and the widow. So will you serve the City.

If you ask me which of all these things is the most important, I reply that among them there is only one thing of superlative importance and that is *yourself*. By far the greatest thing a man can do for his City is to be a good man. Simply to live there as a good man, as a Christian man of action and practical citizen, is the first and highest contribution any one can make to its salvation. Let a City be a Sodom or a Gomorrah, and if there be but ten righteous men in it, it will be saved.

It is here that the older, the more individual, conception of Christianity, did such mighty work for the world—it produced good men. It is goodness that tells, goodness first and goodness last. Good men even with small views are immeasurably more important to the world than small men with great views. But given good men, such men as were produced even by the self-centred theology of an older generation, and add that wider outlook and social ideal which are coming to be the characteristic of the religion of this age, and Christianity has an equipment for the reconstruction of the world, before which nothing can stand. Such good men will not merely content themselves with being good men. They will be forces—according to their measure, public forces. They will take the City in hand, some a house, some a street, and some the whole. Of set purpose they will serve. Not ostentatiously, but silently, in ways varied as human nature, and many as life's opportunities, they will minister to its good.

To help the people, also, to be good people—

good fathers, and mothers, and sons, and citizens—
is worth all else rolled into one. Arrange the
government of the City as you may, perfect all its
philanthropic machinery, make righteous its relations great and small, equip it with galleries and
parks, and libraries and music, and carry out the
whole programme of social reform, and the one
thing needful is still without the gates. The gospel
of material blessedness is part of a gospel—a great
and Christian part—but when held up as the whole
gospel for the people it is as hollow as the void of
life whose circumference even it fails to touch

There are countries in the world—new countries
—where the people, rising to the rights of government, have already secured almost all that reformers
cry for. The lot of the working man there is all but
perfect. His wages are high, his leisure great, his
home worthy. Yet in tens of thousands of cases
the secret of life is unknown.

It is idle to talk of Christ as a social reformer if
by that is meant that His first concern was to
improve the organisation of society, or provide
the world with better laws. These were among His
objects, but His first was to provide the world with
better men. The one need of every cause and every
community still is for better men. If every workshop held a Workman like Him who worked in the

carpenter's shop at Nazareth, the labour problem and all other workman's problems would soon be solved. If every street had a home or two like Mary's home in Bethany, the domestic life of the city would be transformed in three generations.

External reforms—education, civilisation, public schemes, and public charities—have each their part to play. Any experiment that can benefit by one hairbreadth any single human life is a thousand times worth trying. There is no effort in any single one of these directions but must, as Christianity advances, be pressed by Christian men to ever further and fuller issues. But those whose hands have tried the most, and whose eyes have seen the furthest, have come back to regard first the deeper evangel of individual lives, and the philanthropy of quiet ways, and the slow work of leavening men one by one with the spirit of Jesus Christ.

The thought that the future, that any day, may see some new and mighty enterprise of redemption, some new departure in religion, which shall change everything with a breath and make all that is crooked straight, is not at all likely to be realised. There is nothing wrong with the lines on which redemption runs at present except the want of faith to believe in them, and the want of men to use them. The Kingdom of God is like leaven, and the leaven is with us now. The quantity at work in the world may increase but that is all. For nothing can ever be higher than the Spirit of Christ or more potent as a regenerating power on the lives of men.

Do not charge me with throwing away my brief because I return to this old, old plea for the individual soul. I do not forget that my plea is for the City. But I plead for good men, because good men are good leaven. If their goodness stop short of that, if the leaven does not mix with that which is unleavened, if it does not do the work of leaven— that is, to *raise something*—it is not the leaven of Christ. The question for good men to ask themselves is : Is my goodness helping others ? Is it a private luxury, or is it telling upon the City ? Is it bringing any single human soul nearer happiness or righteousness ?

If you ask what particular scheme you shall take up, I cannot answer. Christianity has no set schemes. It makes no choice between conflicting philanthropies, decides nothing between competing churches, favours no particular public policy, organises no one line of private charity. It is not essential even for all of us to take any public or formal line. Christianity is not all carried on by

Committees, and the Kingdom of God has other
ways of coming than through municipal reforms.
Most of the stones for the buildings of the City of
God, and all the best of them, are made by
mothers. But whether or no you shall work through
public channels, or only serve Christ along the
quieter paths of home, no man can determine but
yourself.

There is an almost awful freedom about Christ's
religion. " I do not call you servants," He said,
" for the servant knoweth not what his lord doeth.
I have called you friends." As Christ's friends,
His followers are supposed to know what He wants
done, and for the same reason they will try to do
it—this is the whole working basis of Christianity.
Surely next to its love for the chief of sinners the
most touching thing about the religion of Christ
is its amazing trust in the least of saints. Here is
the mightiest enterprise ever launched upon this
earth, mightier even than its creation, for it is
its re-creation, and the carrying of it out is left,
so to speak, to haphazard—to individual loyalty,
to free enthusiasms, to uncoerced activities, to an
uncompelled response to the pressures of God's
Spirit.

Christ sets His followers no tasks. He appoints
no hours. He allots no sphere. He Himself simply

went about and did good. He did not stop life to do some special thing which should be called religious. His life was His religion. Each day as it came brought round in the ordinary course its natural ministry. Each village along the highway had someone waiting to be helped. His pulpit was the hillside, His congregation a woman at a well. The poor, wherever He met them, were His clients ; the sick, as often as He found them, His opportunity. His work was everywhere ; His workshop was the world. One's associations of Christ are all of the wayside. We never think of Him in connection with a Church. We cannot picture Him in the garb of a priest or belonging to any of the classes who specialise religion. His service was of a universal human order. He was the Son of Man, the Citizen.

This, remember, was the highest life ever lived, this informal citizen-life. So simple a thing it was, so natural, so human, that those who saw it first did not know it was religion, and Christ did not pass among them as a very religious man. Nay, it is certain, and it is an infinitely significant thought, that the religious people of His time not only refused to accept this type of religion as any kind of religion at all, but repudiated and denounced Him as its bitter enemy.

Inability to discern what true religion is, is not confined to the Pharisees. Multitudes still who profess to belong to the religion of Christ, scarcely know it when they see it. The truth is, men will hold to almost anything in the name of Christianity, believe anything, do anything—except its common and obvious tasks. Great is the mystery of what has passed in this world for religion.

I SAW NO TEMPLE THERE

" I SAW no Church there," said John. Nor is there any note of surprise as he marks the omission of what one half of Christendom would have considered the first essential. For beside the type of religion he had learned from Christ, the Church type—the merely Church type—is an elaborate evasion. What have the pomp and circumstance, the fashion and the form, the vestures and the postures, to do with Jesus of Nazareth ? At a stage in personal development, and for a certain type of mind, such things may have a place. But when mistaken for Christianity, no matter how they aid it, or in what measure they conserve it, they defraud the souls of men, and rob humanity of its dues. It is because to large masses of people Christianity has become synonymous with a Temple service that other large masses of people decline to touch it. It is a mistake to suppose that the working classes of this country are opposed to Christianity. No man can ever be opposed to Christianity who knows what it *really* is. The working men would still follow Christ if He came among them. As a matter of fact they do follow anyone, preacher or layman, in pulpit or on platform, who is the least like Him. But what they cannot follow, and must evermore live outside of, is a worship which ends with the worshipper, a religion expressed only in ceremony, and a faith unrelated to life.

Perhaps the most dismal fact of history is the failure of the great organised bodies of ecclesiasticism to understand the simple genius of Christ's religion. Whatever the best in the Churches of all time may have thought of the life and religion of Christ, taken as a whole they have succeeded in leaving upon the mind of a large portion of the world an impression of Christianity which is the direct opposite of the reality. Down to the present hour almost whole nations in Europe live, worship, and die under the belief that Christ is an ecclesiastical Christ, religion the sum of all the Churches' observances, and faith an adhesion to the Churches' creeds. I do not apportion blame ; I simply record the fact. Everything that the spiritual and temporal authority of man could do has been done —done in ignorance of the true nature of Christianity—to dislodge the religion of Christ from its natural home in the heart of Humanity. In many lands the Churches have literally stolen Christ from the people ; they have made the Son of Man the Priest of an Order ; they have taken Christianity from the City and imprisoned it behind altar rails ; they have withdrawn it from the national life and doled it out to the few who pay to keep the unconscious deception up.

Do not do the Church, the true Church at least, the injustice to think that she does not know all this. Nowhere, not even in the fiercest secular press, is there more exposure of this danger, more indignation at its continuance, than in many of the Churches of to-day. The protest against the confusion of Christianity with the Church is the most threadbare of pulpit themes. Before the University of Oxford, from the pulpit of St. Mary's, these words were lately spoken : " If it is strange that the Church of the darker ages should have needed so bitter a lesson (the actual demolition of their churches), is it not ten times stranger still that the Church of the days of greater enlightenment should be found again making the chief part of its business the organising of the modes of worship; that the largest efforts which are owned as the efforts of the Church are made for the establishment and maintenance of worship; that our chief controversies relate to the teaching and the ministry of a system designed primarily, if not exclusively, for worship; that even the fancies and the refinements of such a system divide us; that the breach between things secular and things religious grows wider instead of their being made to blend into one; and that the vast and fruitful spaces of the actual life of mankind lie still so largely without the gates? The old Jerusalem was all temple. The mediæval Church was all temple. But the ideal of the new Jerusalem was—no temple, but a God-inhabited society. Are we not reversing this ideal in an age when the Church still means in so many mouths the clergy, instead of meaning the Christian society, and when nine men are striving to get men to go to church for one who is striving to make men realise that they themselves are the Church?"

Yet even with words so strong as these echoing daily from Protestant pulpits the superstition reigns in all but unbroken power. And everywhere still men are found confounding the spectacular services of a Church, the vicarious religion of a priest, and the traditional belief in a creed, with the living religion of the Son of Man.

"I saw no Temple there"—the future City will be a City without a Church. Ponder that fact, realise the temporariness of the Church, then—go and build one. Do not imagine, because all this has been said, that I mean to depreciate the Church. On the contrary, if it were mine to build a City, a City where all life should be religious, and all men destined to become members of the Body of Christ, the first stone I should lay there would be the foundation-stone of a Church. Why? Because, among other reasons, the product which the Church on the whole best helps to develop, and in the largest quantity, is that which is most needed by the City.

For the present, and for a long time to come, the manufactory of good men, the nursery of the forces which are to redeem the City, will in the main be found to be some more or less formal, more or less imperfect, Christian Church. Here and there an unchurched soul may stir the multitudes to lofty deeds; isolated men, strong enough to preserve their souls apart from the Church, but short-sighted enough perhaps to fail to see that others cannot, may set high examples and stimulate

to national reforms. But for the rank and file of us, made of such stuff as we are made of, the steady pressures of fixed institutions, the regular diets of a common worship, and the education of public Christian teaching are too obvious safeguards of spiritual culture to be set aside. Even Renan declares his conviction that " Beyond the family and outside the State, man has need of the Church.
. . . Civil society, whether it calls itself a commune, a canton, or a province, a state, or fatherland, has many duties towards the improvement of the individual ; but what it does is necessarily limited. The family ought to do much more, but often it is insufficient ; sometimes it is wanting altogether. The association created in the name of moral principle can alone give to every man coming into this world a bond which unites him with the past, duties as to the future, examples to follow, a heritage to receive and to transmit, and a tradition of devotion to continue." Apart altogether from the quality of its contribution to society, in the mere quantity of the work it turns out its stands alone. Even for social purposes the Church is by far the greatest Employment Bureau in the world. And the man who, seeing where it falls short, withholds on that account his witness to its usefulness, is a traitor to history and to fact.

" The Church," as the preacher whom I have already quoted most truly adds, " is a society which tends to embrace the whole life of mankind, to bind all their relations together by a Divine sanction. As such, it blends naturally with the institutions of common life—those institutions which, because they are natural and necessary, are therefore Divine. What it aims at is not the recognition by the nation of a worshipping body, governed by the ministers of public worship, which calls itself the Church, but that the nation and all classes in it should act upon Christian principle, that laws should be made in Christ's spirit of justice, that the relations of the powers of the state should be maintained on a basis of Christian equity, that all public acts should be done in Christ's spirit, and with mutual forbearance, that the spirit of Christian charity should be spread through all ranks and orders of the people. The Church will maintain public worship as one of the greatest supports of a Christian public life ; but it will always remember that the true service is a life of devotion to God and man far more than the common utterance of prayer "

I have said that were it mine to build a City, the first stone I should lay there would be the foundation-stone of a Church. But if it were mine to preach the first sermon in that Church, I should choose as the text, " I saw no Church therein." I should tell the people that the great use of the Church is to help men to do without it. As the old ecclesiastical term has it, Church services are " diets " of worship. They are meals. All who are hungry will take them, and, if they are wise, regularly. But no workman is paid for his meals. He is paid for the work he does in the strength of them. No Christian is paid for going to Church. He goes there for a meal, for strength from God and from his fellow-worshippers to do the work of life —which is the work of Christ. The Church is a Divine institution because it is so very human an institution. As a channel of nourishment, as a stimulus to holy deeds, as a link with all holy lives, let all men use it, and to the utmost of their opportunity. But by all that they know of Christ or care for man, let them beware of mistaking its services for Christianity. What Church services really express is the *want* of Christianity. And when that which is perfect in Christianity is come, all this, as the mere passing stay and scaffolding of struggling souls, must vanish away

If the masses who never go to Church only knew that the Churches were the mute expression of a Christian's *wants* and not the self-advertisement of his sanctity, they would have more respectful words for Churches. But they have never learned this. And the result in their case of confounding religion with the Church is even more serious than in the case of the professing Christian. When they break with the Church it means to them a break with all religion. As things are it could scarce be otherwise. With the Church in ceaseless evidence before their eyes as the acknowledged custodian of Christianity; with actual stone and lime in every street representing the place where religion dwells; with a professional class moving out and in among them holding in their hands the souls of men, and almost the keys of Heaven—how is it possible that those who turn their backs on all this should not feel outcast from the Church's God? It is not possible. Without a murmur, yet with results to themselves most disastrous and pathetic, multitudes accept this false dividing-line and number themselves as excommunicate from all good. The masses will never return to the Church till its true relation to the City is more defined. And they can never have that most real life of theirs made religious so long as they rule themselves out of court on the ground that they have broken with ecclesiastical forms. The life of the masses is the most real of all lives. It is full of religious possibilities. Every movement

of it and every moment of it might become of supreme
religious value, might hold a continuous spiritual
discipline, might perpetuate, and that in most
natural ways, a moral influence which should
pervade all Cities and all States. But they must
first be taught what Christianity really is, and learn
to distinguish between religion and the Church.
After that, if they be taught their lesson well,
they will return to honour both.

Our fathers made much of " meetness " for
Heaven. By prayer and fasting, by self-examination and meditation they sought to fit themselves
" for the inheritance of the saints in light." Important beyond measure in their fitting place are
these exercises of the soul. But whether alone they
fit men for the inheritance of the saints depends
on what a saint is. If a saint is a devotee and not
a citizen, if Heaven is a cathedral and not a City,
then these things do fit for Heaven. But if life
means action, and Heaven service ; if spiritual
graces are acquired for use and not for ornament,
then devotional forms have a deeper function. The
Puritan preachers were wont to tell their people to
" practise dying." Yes ; but what is dying ?
It is going to a City. And what is required of those
who would go to a City ? The practice of Citizenship—the due employment of the unselfish talents,

the development of public spirit, the payment of the full tax to the great brotherhood, the subordination of personal aims to the common good. And where are these to be learned ? Here ; in Cities here. There is no other way to learn them. There is no Heaven to those who have not learned them.

No Church however holy, no priest however earnest, no book however sacred, can transfer to any human character the capacities of Citizenship— those capacities which in the very nature of things are *necessities* to those who would live in the kingdom of God. The only preparation which multitudes seem to make for Heaven is for its Judgment Bar. What will they do in its streets ? What have they learned of Citizenship. What have they practised of love ? How like are they to its Lord ? To " practise dying " is to practise living. Earth is the rehearsal for Heaven. The eternal beyond is the eternal here. The street-life, the home-life, the business-life, the City-life in all the varied range of its activity, are an apprenticeship for the City of God. There is no other apprenticeship for it. To know how to serve Christ in these is to " practise dying."

To move among the people on the common street ; to meet them in the market-place on equal terms ; to live among them not as saint or monk, but as brother-man with brother-man; to serve God not with form or ritual, but in the free impulse of a soul; to bear the burden of society and relieve its needs; to carry on the multitudinous activities of the City—social, commercial, political, philanthropic—in Christ's spirit and for His ends: this is the religion of the Son of Man, and the only meetness for Heaven which has much reality in it.

No; the Church with all its splendid equipment, the cloister with all its holy opportunity, are not the final instruments for fitting men for Heaven. The City, in many of its functions, is a greater Church than the Church. It is amid the whirr of its machinery and in the discipline of its life that the souls of men are really made. How great its opportunity is we are few of us aware. It is such slow work getting better, the daily round is so very common, our ideas of a heavenly life are so unreal and mystical that even when the highest Heaven lies all around us, when we might touch it, and dwell in it every day we live, we almost fail to see that it is there. The Heaven of our childhood, the spectacular Heaven, the Heaven which is a *place*, so dominates thought even in our maturer years, that we are slow to learn the fuller truth that Heaven is a *state*. But John, who is responsible before all other teachers for the dramatic view of

Heaven, has not failed in this very allegory to proclaim the further lesson. Having brought all his scenery upon the stage and pictured a material Heaven of almost unimaginable splendour, the seer turns aside before he closes for a revelation of a profounder kind. Within the Heavenly City he opens the gate of an inner Heaven. It is the spiritual Heaven—the Heaven of those who serve. With two flashes of his pen he tells the Citizens of God all that they will ever need or care to know as to what Heaven really means. " His servants shall serve Him ; and *they shall see His Face ; and His Character shall be written on their characters.*"

They shall see His Face. Where ? In the City. When ? In Eternity ? No ; to-morrow. Those who serve in any City cannot help continually seeing Christ. He is there with them. He is there before them. They cannot but meet. No gentle word is ever spoken that Christ's voice does not also speak ; no meek deed is ever done that the unsummoned Vision does not there and then appear. Whoso, in whatsoever place, receiveth a little child in My name receiveth Me.

This is how men get to know God—by doing His will. And there is no other way. And this is how men become like God ; how God's character becomes written upon men's characters. Acts react upon souls. Good acts make good men ; just acts, just men ; kind acts, kind men ; divine acts, divine men. And there is no other way of becoming good, just, kind, divine. And there is no Heaven for those who have not become these. For these are Heaven.

When John's Heaven faded from his sight, and the prophet woke to the desert waste of Patmos, did he grudge to exchange the Heaven of his dream for the common tasks around him ? Was he not glad to be alive, and there ? And would he not straightway go to the City, to whatever struggling multitude his prison-rock held, if so be that he might prove his dream and among them see His Face ? Traveller to God's last City, be glad that you are alive. Be thankful for the City at your door and for the chance to build its walls a little nearer Heaven before you go. Pray for yet a little while to redeem the wasted years. And week by week as you go forth from worship, and day by day as you awake to face this great and needy world, learn to " seek a City " there, and in the service of its neediest citizen find Heaven.

IV.

THE CHANGED LIFE

We all
With unveiled face
Reflecting
As a Mirror
The Glory of the Lord
Are transformed
Into the same image
From Glory to Glory
Even as from the Lord
The Spirit.

THE CHANGED LIFE

" I PROTEST that if some great power would agree to make me always think what is true and do what is right, on condition of being turned into a sort of clock and wound up every morning, I should instantly close with the offer."

THESE are the words of Mr. Huxley. The infinite desirability, the infinite difficulty of being good—the theme is as old as humanity. The man does not live from whose deeper being the same confession has not risen, or who would not give his all to-morrow, if he could " close with the offer " of becoming a better man.

I propose to make that offer now. In all seriousness, without being " turned into a sort of clock," the end can be attained. Under the right conditions it is as natural for character to become beautiful as for a flower ; and if on God's earth, there is not some machinery for effecting it, the supreme gift to the world has been forgotten. This is simply what man was made for. With Browning : " I say that Man was made to grow, not stop." Or in the deeper words of an older Book : " Whom He did foreknow, He also did predestinate . . . **to be** conformed to the Image of his Son."

Let me begin by naming, and in part discarding, some processes in vogue already, for producing better lives. These processes are far from wrong ; in their place they may even be essential. One ventures to disparage them only because they do not turn out the most perfect possible work.

The first imperfect method is to rely on Resolution. In will-power, in mere spasms of earnestness there is no salvation. Struggle, effort, even agony, have their place in Christianity as we shall see ; but this is not where they come in. In mid-Atlantic the other day, the *Etruria*, in which I was sailing, suddenly stopped. Something had gone wrong with the engines. There were five hundred able-bodied men on board the ship. Do you think if we had gathered together and pushed against the masts we could have pushed it on ? When one attempts to sanctify himself by effort, he is trying to make his boat go by pushing against the mast. He is like a drowning man trying to lift himself out of the water by pulling at the hair of his own head. Christ held up this method almost **to** ridicule when He said, " Which of you by taking thought can add a cubit to his stature ? " The one redeeming feature of the self-sufficient method is this—that those who try it find out almost at once that it will not gain the goal.

Another experimenter says :—" But that is not my method. I have seen the folly of a mere wild struggle in the dark. I work on a principle. My plan is not to waste power on random effort, but to concentrate on a single sin. By taking one at a time and crucifying it steadily, I hope in the end to extirpate all." To this, unfortunately, there are four objections. For one thing life is too short ; the name of sin is Legion. For another thing, to deal with individual sins is to leave the rest of the nature for the time untouched. In the third place, a single combat with a special sin does not affect the root and spring of the disease. If one only of the channels of sin be obstructed, experience points to an almost certain overflow through some other part of the nature. Partial conversion is almost always accompanied by such moral leakage, for the pent-up energies accumulate to the bursting point, and the last state of that soul may be worse than the first. In the last place, religion does not consist in negatives, in stopping this sin and stopping that. The perfect character can never be produced with a pruning knife.

But a third protests :—" So be it. I make no attempt to stop sins one by one. My method is

just the opposite. I copy the virtues one by one."
The difficulty about the copying method is that it is
apt to be mechanical. One can always tell an
engraving from a picture, an artificial flower from
a real flower. To copy virtues one by one has
somewhat the same effect as eradicating the vices
one by one; the temporary result is an over-
balanced and incongruous character. Someone
defines a *prig* as " a creature that is over-fed for
its size." One sometimes finds Christians of this
species—over-fed on one side of their nature, but
dismally thin and starved-looking on the other.
The result, for instance, of copying Humility, and
adding it on to an otherwise worldly life, is simply
grotesque. A rabid Temperance advocate, for the
same reason, is often the poorest of creatures,
flourishing on a single virtue, and quite oblivious
that his Temperance is making a worse man of him
and not a better. These are examples of fine virtues
spoiled by association with mean companions.
Character is a unity, and all the virtues must
advance together to make the perfect man. This
method of sanctification, nevertheless, is in the
true direction. It is only in the details of execution
that it fails.

A fourth method I need scarcely mention, for it
is a variation on those already named. It is the

very young man's method ; and the pure earnestness of it makes it almost desecration to touch it. It is to keep a private note-book with columns for the days of the week, and a list of virtues with spaces against each for marks. This, with many stern rules for preface, is stored away in a secret place, and from time to time, at nightfall, the soul is arraigned before it as before a private judgment bar. This living by code was Franklin's method ; and I suppose thousands more could tell how they had hung up in their bed-rooms, or hid in lock-fast drawers, the rules which one solemn day they drew up to shape their lives. This method is not erroneous, only somehow its success is poor. You bear me witness that it fails ? And it fails generally for very matter-of-fact reasons—most likely because one day we forget the rules.

All these methods that have been named—the self-sufficient method, the self-crucifixion method, the mimetic method, and the diary method—are perfectly human, perfectly natural, perfectly ignorant, and, as they stand, perfectly inadequate. It is not argued, I repeat, that they must be abandoned. Their harm is rather that they distract attention from the true working method, and secure a fair result at the expense of the perfect one. What that perfect method is we shall now go on to ask.

THE FORMULA OF SANCTIFICATION

A FORMULA, a receipt, for Sanctification—can one seriously speak of this mighty change as if the process were as definite as for the production of so many volts of electricity? It is impossible to doubt it. Shall a mechanical experiment succeed infallibly, and the one vital experiment of humanity remain a chance? Is corn to grow by method, and character by caprice? If we cannot calculate to a certainty that the forces of religion will do their work, then is religion vain. And if we cannot express the law of these forces in simple words, then is Christianity not the world's religion but the world's conundrum.

Where, then, shall one look for such a formula. Where one would look for any formula—among the text books. And if we turn to the text books of Christianity we shall find a formula for this problem as clear and precise as any in the mechanical sciences. If this simple rule, moreover, be but followed fearlessly, it will yield the result of a perfect character as surely as any result that is guaranteed by the laws of nature. The finest expression of this rule in Scripture, or indeed in any literature, is probably one drawn up and condensed into a single verse by Paul. You will find it in a letter—the second to the Corinthians—written by him to some Christian people who, in a city which was a byword for depravity and licentiousness, were seeking the higher life. To see the point of the words we must take them from the immensely improved rendering of the Revised translation, for the older Version in this case greatly obscures the sense. They are these : " we all, with unveiled face reflecting as a mirror the glory of the Lord, are transformed into the same image from glory to glory, even as from the Lord the Spirit."

Now observe at the outset the entire contradiction of all our previous efforts, in the simple passive, " we *are* transformed." We *are changed*, as the Old Version has it—we do not change ourselves. No man can change himself. Throughout the New Testament you will find that wherever these moral and spiritual transformations are described the verbs are in the passive. Presently it will be pointed out that there is a *rationale* in this ; but meantime do not toss these words aside as if this passivity denied all human effort or ignored intelligible law. What is implied for the soul here is no more than is everywhere claimed for the body. In physiology the verbs describing the processes of growth are in the passive.~ Growth is not voluntary ; it takes place, it happens, it is wrought upon matter. So here. " Ye must be born again "—we cannot *born* ourselves. " Be not conformed to this world but *be ye transformed* "—we are subjects to a transforming influence, we do not transform ourselves. Not more certain is it that it is something outside the thermometer that produces a change in the thermometer, than it is something outside the soul of man that produces a moral change upon him. That he must be susceptible to that change, that he must be a party to it goes without saying ; but that neither his aptitude nor his will can produce it, is equally certain.

Obvious as it ought to seem, this may be to some an almost startling revelation. The change we have been striving after is not to be produced by any more striving after. It is to be wrought upon us by the moulding of hands beyond our own. As the branch ascends, and the bud bursts, and the fruit reddens under the co-operation of influences from the outside air, so man rises to the higher stature under invisible pressures from without. The radical defect of all our former methods of sanctification was the attempt to generate from within that which can only be wrought upon us from without. According to the

first Law of Motion : Every body continues in its
state of rest, or of uniform motion in a straight
line, except in so far as it may be compelled *by
impressed forces* to change that state. This is
also a first law of Christianity. Every man's
character remains as it is, or continues in the
direction in which it is going, until it is compelled
by impressed forces to change that state. Our failure
has been the failure to put ourselves in the way of
the impressed forces. There is a clay, and there is
a Potter ; we have tried to get the clay to mould
the clay.

Whence, then, these pressures, and where this
Potter ? The answer of the formula is " By reflecting as a mirror the glory of the Lord we are
changed." But this is not very clear. What is the
" glory " of the Lord, and how can mortal man
reflect it, and how can that act as an " impressed
force " in moulding him to a nobler form ? The
word " glory "—the word which has to bear the
weight of holding those " impressed forces "—is
a stranger in current speech, and our first duty
is to seek out its equivalent in working English.
It suggests at first a radiance of some kind, something dazzling or glittering, some halo such as
the old masters loved to paint round the heads of
their Ecce Homos. But that is paint, mere matter,

the visible symbol of some unseen thing. What is that unseen thing? It is that of all unseen things, the most radiant, the most beautiful, the most Divine, and that is *Character*. On earth, in Heaven, there is nothing so great, so glorious as this. The word has many meanings; in ethics it can have but one. Glory is character and nothing less, and it can be nothing more. The earth is " full of the glory of the Lord," because it is full of His character. The " Beauty of the Lord " is character. " The effulgence of His Glory " is character. " The Glory of the Only Begotten " is character, the character which is " fulness of grace and truth." And when God told His people *His name* He simply gave them His character, His character which was Himself : " And the Lord proclaimed the Name of the Lord . . . the Lord, the Lord God, merciful and gracious, long-suffering and abundant in goodness and truth." Glory then is not something intangible, or ghostly, or transcendental. If it were this how could Paul ask men to reflect it? Stripped of its physical enswathement it is Beauty, moral and spiritual Beauty, Beauty infinitely real, infinitely exalted, yet infinitely near and infinitely communicable.

With this explanation read over the sentence once more in paraphrase : We all reflecting as a mirror the character of Christ are transformed into the same Image from character to character—from a poor character to a better one, from a better one to one a little better still, from that to one still more complete, until by slow degrees the Perfect Image is attained. Here the solution of the problem of sanctification is compressed into a sentence : Reflect the character of Christ and you will become like Christ.

All men are mirrors—that is the first law on which this formula is based. One of the aptest descriptions of a human being is that he is a mirror. As we sat at table to-night the world in which each of us lived and moved throughout this day was focussed in the room. What we saw as we looked at one another was not one another, but one another's world. We were an arrangement of mirrors. The scenes we saw were all reproduced ; the people we met walked to and fro ; they spoke, they bowed, they passed us by, did everything over again as if it had been real. When we talked, we were but looking at our own mirror and describing what flitted across it ; our listening was not hearing, but seeing—we but looked on our neighbour's mirror. All human intercourse is a seeing of reflections. I meet a stranger in a railway carriage. The cadence of his first word tells me he is English, and comes from Yorkshire. Without knowing it he has reflected his birthplace, his parents, and the long history of their race. Even physiologically he is a mirror. His second sentence records that he is a politician, and a faint inflexion in the way he pronounces *The Times* reveals his party. In his next remarks I see reflected a whole world of experiences. The books he has read, the people he has met, the influences that have played upon him and made him the man he is—these are all registered there by a pen which lets nothing pass, and whose writing can never be blotted out. What I am reading in him meantime he also is reading in me ; and before the journey is over we could half write each other's lives. Whether we like it or not, we live in glass houses. The mind, the memory, the soul, is simply a vast chamber panelled with looking-glass. And upon this miraculous arrangement and endowment depends the capacity of mortal souls to " reflect the character of the Lord."

But this is not all. If all these varied reflections from our so-called secret life are patent to the world, how close the writing, how complete the record, within the soul itself ? For the influences we meet are not simply held for a moment on the polished surface and thrown off again into space. Each is retained where first it fell, and stored up in the soul for ever.

This law of Assimilation is the second, and by far the most impressive truth which underlies the formula of sanctification—the truth that men are not only mirrors, but that these mirrors so far from being mere reflectors of the fleeting things they see, transfer into their own inmost substance, and hold in permanent preservation the things that they reflect. No one knows how the soul can hold these things. No one knows how the miracle is done. No phenomenon in nature, no process in chemistry, no chapter in necromancy can even help us to begin to understand this amazing operation. For, think of it, the past is not only focussed there, in a man's soul, it *is* there. How could it be reflected from there if it were not there? All things that he has ever seen, known, felt, believed of the surrounding world are now within him, have become part of him, in part are him—he has been changed into their image. He may deny it, he may resent it, but they are there. They do not adhere to him, they are transfused through him. He cannot alter or rub them out. They are not in his memory, they are in *him*. His soul is as they have filled it, made it, left it. These things, these books, these events, these influences are his makers. In their hands are life and death, beauty and deformity. When once the image or likeness of any of these is fairly presented to the soul, no power on earth can hinder two things happening—it must be absorbed into the soul and for ever reflected back again from character.

Upon these astounding yet perfectly obvious Psychological facts, Paul bases his doctrine of sanctification. He sees that character is a thing built up by slow degrees, that it is hourly changing for better or for worse according to the images which flit across it. One step further and the whole length and breadth of the application of these ideas to the central problem of religion will stand before us.

THE ALCHEMY OF INFLUENCE

IF events change men, much more persons. No man can meet another on the street without making some mark upon him. We say we exchange words when we meet ; what we exchange is souls. And when intercourse is very close and very frequent, so complete is this exchange that recognisable bits of the one soul begin to show in the other's nature, and the second is conscious of a similar and growing debt to the first. This mysterious approximating of two souls who has not witnessed ? Who has not watched some old couple come down life's pilgrimage hand in hand with such gentle trust and joy in one another that their very faces wore the self-same look ? These were not two souls ; it was a composite soul. It did not matter to which of the two you spoke, you would have said the same words to either. It was quite indifferent which replied, each would have said the same. Half a century's *reflecting* had told upon them : they were changed into the same image. It is the Law of Influence that *we become like those whom we habitually admire :* these had become like because they habitually admired. Through all the range of literature, of history, and biography this law presides. Men are all mosaics of other men. There was a savour of David about Jonathan and a savour of Jonathan about David. Jean Valjean, in the masterpiece of Victor Hugo, is Bishop Bienvenu risen from the dead. Metempsychosis is a fact. George Eliot's message to the world was that men and women make men and women. The Family, the cradle of mankind, has no meaning apart from this. Society itself is nothing but a rallying point for these omnipotent forces to do their work. On the doctrine of Influence, in short, the whole vast pyramid of humanity is built

But it was reserved for Paul to make the supreme application of the Law of Influence. It was a tremendous inference to make, but he never hesitated. He himself was a changed man : he knew exactly what had done it ; it was Christ. On the Damascus road they met, and from that hour his life was absorbed in His. The effect could not but follow—on words, on deeds, on career, on creed. The " impressed forces " did their vital work. He became like Him whom he habitually loved. " So we all," he writes, " reflecting as a mirror the glory of Christ are changed into the same image."

Nothing could be more simple, more intelligible, more natural, more supernatural. It is an analogy from an everyday fact. Since we are what we are by the impacts of those who surround us, those who surround themselves with the highest will be those who change into the highest. There are some men and some women in whose company we are always at our best. While with them we cannot think mean thoughts or speak ungenerous words. Their mere presence is elevation, purification, sanctity. All the best stops in our nature are drawn out by their intercourse, and we find a music in our souls that was never there before. Suppose even *that* influence prolonged through a month, a year, a lifetime, and what could not life become ? Here, even on the common plane of life, talking our language, walking our streets, working side by side, are sanctifiers of souls ; here, breathing through common clay, is Heaven ; here, energies charged even through a temporal medium with a virtue of regeneration. If to live with men, diluted to the millionth degree with the virtue of the Highest, can exalt and purify the nature, what bounds can be set to the influence of Christ ? To live with Socrates—with unveiled face—must have made one wise ; with Aristides, just. Francis of Assisi must have made one gentle ; Savonarola, strong. But to have lived with Christ ? To have lived with Christ must have made one like Christ ; that is to say, *A Christian*

As a matter of fact, to live with Christ did produce this effect. It produced it in the case of Paul. And during Christ's life-time the experiment was tried in an even more startling form. A few raw, unspiritual, uninspiring men, were admitted to the inner circle of His friendship. The change began at once. Day by day we can almost see the first disciples grow. First there steals over them the faintest possible adumbration of His character, and occasionally, very occasionally, they do a thing, or say a thing that they could not have done or said had they not been living there. Slowly the spell of His Life deepens. Reach after reach of their nature is overtaken, thawed, subjugated, sanctified. Their manners soften, their words become more gentle, their conduct more unselfish. As swallows who have found a summer, as frozen buds the spring, their starved humanity bursts into a fuller life. They do not know how it is, but they are different men. One day they find themselves like their Master, going about and doing good. To themselves it is unaccountable, but they cannot do otherwise. They were not told to do it, it came to them to do it. But the people who watch them know well how to account for it—" They have been," they whisper, " with Jesus." Already even, the mark and seal of His character is upon them—" They have been with Jesus." Unparalleled phenomenon, that these poor fishermen should remind other men of Christ ! Stupendous victory and mystery of regeneration that mortal men should suggest to the world, *God !*

There is something almost melting in the way

His contemporaries, and John especially, speak of the Influence of Christ. John lived himself in daily wonder at Him ; he was overpowered, over-awed, entranced, transfigured. To his mind it was impossible for anyone to come under this influence and ever be the same again. " Whosoever abideth in Him sinneth not," he said. It was inconceivable that he could sin, as inconceivable as that ice should live in a burning sun, or darkness co-exist with noon. If anyone did sin, it was to John the simple proof that he could never have met Christ. " Whosoever sinneth," he exclaims, " hath not seen *Him*, neither known *Him*." Sin was abashed in this Presence. Its roots withered. Its sway and victory were for ever at an end.

But these were His contemporaries. It was easy for *them* to be influenced by Him, for they were every day and all the day together. But how can we mirror that which we have never seen ? How can all this stupendous result be produced by a Memory, by the scantiest of all Biographies, by One who lived and left this earth eighteen hundred years ago ? How can modern men to-day make Christ, the absent Christ, their most constant companion still ? The answer is that Friendship is a spiritual thing. It is independent of Matter, or Space, or Time. That which I love in my friend

is not that which I see What influences me in
my friend is not his body but his spirit It would
have been an ineffable experience truly to have lived
at that time—

" I think when I read the sweet story of old,
    How when Jesus was here among men,
He took little children like lambs to His fold,
    I should like to have been with Him then.

" I wish that His hand had been laid on my head,
    That His arms had been thrown around me,
And that I had seen His kind look when He said,
    ' Let the little ones come unto Me ' "

And yet, if Christ were to come into the world
again few of us probably would ever have a chance
of seeing Him. Millions of her subjects, in this little
country, have never seen their own Queen. And
there would be millions of the subjects of Christ
who could never get within speaking distance of
Him if He were here Our companionship with
Him, like all true companionship, is a spiritual
communion. All friendship, all love, human and
Divine, is purely spiritual. It was after He was
risen that He influenced even the disciples most.
Hence in reflecting the character of Christ it is no

real obstacle that we may never have been in visible contact with Himself.

There lived once a young girl whose perfect grace of character was the wonder of those who knew her She wore on her neck a gold locket which no one was ever allowed to open. One day, in a moment of unusual confidence, one of her companions was allowed to touch its spring and learn its secret. She saw written these words—" *Whom having not seen, I love* " That was the secret of her beautiful life. She had been changed into the Same Image

Now this is not imitation, but a much deeper thing. Mark this distinction. For the difference in the process, as well as in the result, may be as great as that between a photograph secured by the infallible pencil of the sun, and the rude outline from a schoolboy's chalk. Imitation is mechanical, reflection organic. The one is occasional, the other habitual. In the one case, man comes to God and imitates Him ; in the other, God comes to man and imprints Himself upon him. It is quite true that there is an imitation of Christ which amounts to reflection. But Paul's term includes all that the other holds, and is open to no mistake.

" Make Christ your most constant companion " —this is what it practically means for us. Be more under His influence than under any other influence. Ten minutes spent in His society every day, ay, two minutes if it be face to face, and heart to heart, will make the whole day different. Every character has an inward spring, let Christ be it. Every action has a key-note, let Christ set it. Yesterday you got a certain letter. You sat down and wrote a reply which almost scorched the paper. You picked the cruellest adjectives you knew and sent it forth, without a pang, to do its ruthless work. You did that because your life was set in the wrong key. You began the day with the mirror placed at the wrong angle. To-morrow, at daybreak, turn it towards Him, and even to your enemy the fashion of your countenance will be changed. Whatever you then do, one thing you will find you could not do—you could not write that letter. Your first impulse may be the same, your judgment may be unchanged, but if you try it the ink will dry on your pen, and you will rise from your desk an unavenged but a greater and more Christian man. Throughout the whole day your actions, down to the last detail, will do homage to that early vision. Yesterday you thought mostly about yourself. To-day the poor will meet you, and you will feed them. The helpless, the tempted, the sad, will throng about you, and each you will befriend.

Where were all these people yesterday? Where they are to-day, but you did not see them. It is in reflected light that the poor are seen. But your soul to-day is not at the ordinary angle. " Things which are not seen " are visible. For a few short hours you live the Eternal Life. The eternal life, the life of faith, is simply the life of the higher vision. Faith is an attitude—a mirror set at the right angle.

When to-morrow is over, and in the evening you review it, you will wonder how you did it. You will not be conscious that you strove for any-thing, or imitated anything, or crucified any-thing. You will be conscious of Christ ; that He was with you, that without compulsion you were yet compelled, that without force, or noise, or proclamation, the revolution was accomplished. You do not congratulate yourself as one who has done a mighty deed, or achieved a personal success, or stored up a fund of " Christian experience " to ensure the same result again. What you are con-scious of is " the glory of the Lord." And what the world is conscious of, if the result be a true one, is also " the glory of the Lord." In looking at a mirror one does not see the mirror, or think of it, but only of what it reflects. For a mirror never calls atten-tion to itself—except when there are flaws in it.

That this is a real experience and not a vision, that this life is possible to men, is being lived by men to-day, is simple biographical fact. From a thousand witnesses I cannot forbear to summon one. The following are the words of one of the highest intellects this age has known, a man who shares the burdens of his country as few have done, and who, not in the shadows of old age, but in the high noon of his success, gave this confession —I quote it with only a few abridgements—to the world :—

" I want to speak to-night only a little but that little I desire to speak of the sacred name of Christ, who is my life, my inspiration, my hope, and my surety. I cannot help stopping and looking back upon the past. And I wish, as if I had never done it before, to bear witness, not only that it is by the grace of God, but that it is by the grace of God as manifested in Christ Jesus, that I am what I am. I recognise the sublimity and grandeur of the revelation of God in His eternal fatherhood as one that made the heavens, that founded the earth, and that regards all the tribes of the earth, comprehending them in one universal mercy ; but it is the God that is manifested in Jesus Christ, revealed by His life, made

known by the inflections of His feelings, by His
discourse, and by His deeds—it is that God that
I desire to confess to-night, and of whom I desire
to say, " By the love of God in Christ Jesus I
am what I am."

" If you ask me precisely what I mean by that,
I say, frankly, that more than any recognised
influence of my father or my mother upon me ;
more than the social influence of all the members
of my father's household ; more, so far as I can
trace it, or so far as I am made aware of it, than
all the social influences of every kind, Christ has
had the formation of my mind and my disposition.
My hidden ideals of what is beautiful I have drawn
from Christ. My thoughts of what is manly,
and noble, and pure, have almost all of them
arisen from the Lord Jesus Christ. Many men
have educated themselves by reading Plutarch's
Lives of the Ancient Worthies, and setting before
themselves one and another of these that in
different ages have achieved celebrity ; and they
have recognised the great power of these men on
themselves. Now I do not perceive that poet, or
philosopher, or reformer, or general, or any other
great man, ever has dwelt in my imagination
and in my thought as the simple Jesus has.
For more than twenty-five years I instinctively

have gone to Christ to draw a measure and a
rule for everything. Whenever there has been a
necessity for it I have sought—and at last
almost spontaneously—to throw myself into the
companionship of Christ ; and early, by my
imagination, I could see Him standing and looking quietly and lovingly upon me. There seemed
almost to drop from His face an influence upon
me that suggested what was the right thing in
the controlling of passion, in the subduing of pride,
in the overcoming of selfishness ; and it is from
Christ, manifested to my inward eye, that I have
consciously derived more ideals, more models,
more influences, than from any human character
whatever.

" That is not all. I feel conscious that I have
derived from the Lord Jesus Christ every thought
that makes heaven a reality to me, and every
thought that paves the road that lies between me
and heaven. All my conceptions of the progress
of grace in the soul ; all the steps by which divine
life is evolved ; all the ideals that overhang the
blessed sphere which awaits us beyond this world
—these are derived from the Saviour. The life
that I now live in the flesh I live by the faith of
the Son of God.

" That is not all. Much as my future includes

all these elements which go to make the blessed fabric of earthly life, yet, after all, what the summer is compared with all its earthly products —flowers, and leaves, and grass—that is Christ compared with all the products of Christ in my mind and in my soul. All the flowers and leaves of sympathy ; all the twining joys that come from my heart as a Christian—these I take and hold in the future, but they are to me what the flowers and leaves of summer are compared with the sun that makes the summer. Christ is the Alpha and Omega, the beginning and the end of my better life.

" When I read the Bible, I gather a great deal from the Old Testament, and from the Pauline portions of the New Testament ; but after all, I am conscious that the fruit of the Bible is Christ. That is what I read it for, and that is what I find that is worth reading. I have had a hunger to be loved of Christ. You all know, in some relations, what it is to be hungry for love. Your heart seems unsatisfied till you can draw something more toward you from those that are dearest to you. There have been times when I have had an unspeakable heart-hunger for Christ's love. My sense of sin is never strong when I think of the law ; my sense of sin is strong when I think of love—if there is any difference between law and love. It is when drawing near the Lord Jesus Christ, and longing to be loved, that I have the most vivid sense of unsymmetry, of imperfection, of absolute unworthiness, and of my sinfulness. Character and conduct are never so vividly set before me as when in silence I bend in the presence of Christ, revealed not in wrath, but in love to me. I never so much long to be lovely, that I may be loved, as when I have this revelation of Christ before my mind.

" In looking back upon my experience, that part of my life which stands out, and which I remember most vividly, is just that part that has had some conscious association with Christ. All the rest is pale, and thin, and lies like clouds on the horizon. Doctrines, systems, measures, methods—what may be called the necessary mechanical and external part of worship ; the part which the senses would recognise—this seems to have withered and fallen off like leaves of last summer ; but that part which has taken hold of Christ abides."

Can anyone hear this life-music, with its throbbing refrain of Christ, and remain unmoved by envy or desire ? Yet till we have lived like this we have never lived at all

THE FIRST EXPERIMENT

THEN you reduce religion to a common Friendship? A common Friendship—Who talks of a *common* Friendship? There is no such thing in the world. On earth no word is more sublime. Friendship is the nearest thing we know to what religion is. God is love. And to make religion akin to Friendship is simply to give it the highest expression conceivable by man. But if by demurring to "a common friendship" is meant a protest against the greatest and the holiest in religion being spoken of in intelligible terms, then I am afraid the objection is all too real. Men always look for a mystery when one talks of sanctification; some mystery apart from that which must ever be mysterious wherever Spirit works. It is thought some peculiar secret lies behind it, some occult experience which only the initiated know. Thousands of persons go to church every Sunday hoping to solve this mystery. At meetings, at conferences, many a time they have reached what they thought was the very brink of it, but somehow no further revelation came. Poring over religious books, how often were they not within a paragraph of it; the next page, the next sentence, would discover

all, and they would be borne on a flowing tide for
ever But nothing happened. The next sentence
and the next page were read, and still it eluded
them ; and though the promise of its coming kept
faithfully up to the end, the last chapter found them
still pursuing Why did nothing happen ? Because
there was nothing to happen—nothing of the kind
they were looking for Why did it elude them ?
Because there was no " it." When shall we learn
that the pursuit of holiness is simply the pursuit
of Christ ? When shall we substitute for the
" it " of a fictitious aspiration, the approach of
a Living Friend ? Sanctity is in character and
not in moods ; Divinity in our own plain calm
humanity, and in no mystic rapture of the soul

And yet there are others who, for exactly a
contrary reason, will find scant satisfaction here.
Their complaint is not that a religion expressed in
terms of Friendship is too homely, but that it is
still too mystical. To " abide " in Christ, to " make
Christ our most constant companion " is to them
the purest mysticism They want something
absolutely tangible and absolutely direct. These
are not the poetical souls who seek a sign, a
mysticism in excess ; but the prosaic natures
whose want is mathematical definition in details.
Yet it is perhaps not possible to reduce this problem

to much more rigid elements. The beauty of Friendship is its infinity. One can never evacuate life of mysticism. Home is full of it, love is full of it, religion is full of it. Why stumble at that in the relation of man to Christ which is natural in the relation of man to man ?

If anyone cannot conceive or realise a mystical relation with Christ, perhaps all that can be done is to help him to step on to it by still plainer analogies from common life. How do I know Shakespeare or Dante ? By communing with their words and thoughts. Many men know Dante better than their own fathers. He influences them more. As a spiritual presence he is more near to them, as a spiritual force more real. Is there any reason why a greater than Shakespeare or Dante, who also walked this earth, who left great words behind Him, who has great works everywhere in the world now, should not also instruct, inspire, and mould the characters of men ? I do not limit Christ's influence to this. It is this, and it is more. But Christ, so far from resenting or discouraging this relation of Friendship, Himself proposed it. " Abide in Me " was almost His last word to the world. And He partly met the difficulty of those who feel its intangibleness by adding the practical clause, " If ye abide in Me *and My words abide in you.*"

Begin with His words. Words can scarcely ever be long impersonal. Christ Himself was a Word, a word made Flesh. Make His words flesh ; do them, live them, and you must live Christ. "*He that keepeth My commandments*, he it is that loveth Me." Obey Him and you must love Him. Abide in Him and you must obey Him. *Cultivate* His Friendship. Live after Christ, in His Spirit, as in His Presence, and it is difficult to think what more you can do. Take this at least as a first lesson, as introduction. If you cannot at once and always feel the play of His life upon yours, watch for it also indirectly. "The whole earth is full of the character of the Lord." Christ is the Light of the world, and much of His Light is reflected from things in the world—even from clouds. Sunlight is stored in every leaf, from leaf through coal, and it comforts us thence when days are dark and we cannot see the sun. Christ shines through men, through books, through history, through nature, music, art. Look for Him there. "Every day one should either look at a beautiful picture, or hear beautiful music, or read a beautiful poem." The real danger of mysticism is not making it broad enough.

Do not think that nothing is happening because you do not see yourself grow, or hear the whirr of

the machinery. All great things grow noiselessly.
You can see a mushroom grow, but never a child.
Mr. Darwin tells us that Evolution proceeds by
" numerous, successive, and slight modifications."
Paul knew that, and put it, only in more beautiful
words, into the heart of his formula. He said for
the comforting of all slowly perfecting souls that
they grew " from character to character." " The
inward man," he says elsewhere, " is renewed
from day to day." All thorough work is slow ;
all true development by minute slight and insensible metamorphoses. The higher the structure,
moreover, the slower the progress. As the biologist
runs his eye over the long Ascent of Life he sees
the lowest forms of animals develop in an hour ;
the next above these reach maturity in a day ;
those higher still take weeks or months to perfect ;
but the few at the top demand the long experiment
of years. If a child and an ape are born on the same
day the last will be in full possession of its faculties
and doing the active work of life before the child
has left its cradle. Life is the cradle of eternity.
As the man is to the animal in the slowness of his
evolution, so is the spiritual man to the natural
man. Foundations which have to bear the
weight of an eternal life must be surely laid.
Character is to wear for ever ; who will wonder

or grudge that it cannot be developed in a day ?

To await the growing of a soul, nevertheless, is an almost Divine act of faith. How pardonable, surely, the impatience of deformity with itself, of a consciously despicable character standing before Christ, wondering, yearning, hungering to be like that ? Yet must one trust the process fearlessly, and without misgiving. " The Lord the Spirit " will do His part. The tempting expedient is, in haste for abrupt or visible progress, to try some method less spiritual, or to defeat the end by watching for effects instead of keeping the eye on the Cause. A photograph prints from the negative only while exposed to the sun. While the artist is looking to see how it is getting on he simply stops the getting on. Whatever of wise supervision the soul may need, it is certain it can never be over-exposed, or, that, being exposed, anything else in the world can improve the result or quicken it. The creation of a new heart, the renewing of a right spirit is an omnipotent work of God. Leave it to the Creator. " He which hath begun a good work in you will perfect it unto that day "

No man, nevertheless, who feels the worth and solemnity of what is at stake will be careless as to his progress. To become like Christ is the only

thing in the world worth caring for, the thing
before which every ambition of man is folly,
and all lower achievement vain. Those only who
make this quest the supreme desire and passion of
their lives can even begin to hope to reach it. If,
therefore, it has seemed up to this point as if all
depended on passivity, let me now assert, with
conviction more intense, that all depends on
activity. A religion of effortless adoration may be
a religion for an angel but never for a man. Not
in the contemplative, but in the active lies true
life ; not in the realm of ideals but among tangible
things is man's sanctification wrought. Resolution,
effort, pain, self-crucifixion, agony—all the things
already dismissed as futile in themselves must now
be restored to office, and a tenfold responsibility
laid upon them. For what is their office ? Nothing
less than to move the vast inertia of the soul, and
place it, and keep it where the spiritual forces will
act upon it. It is to rally the forces of the will,
and keep the surface of the mirror bright, and ever
in position. It is to uncover the face which is to
look at Christ, and draw down the veil when un-
hallowed sights are near. You have, perhaps,
gone with an astronomer to watch him photograph
the spectrum of a star. As you entered the dark
vault of the Observatory you saw him begin by

lighting a candle. To see the star with? No;
but to see to adjust the instrument to see the star
with. It was the star that was going to take the
photograph; it was, also, the astronomer. For a
long time he worked in the dimness, screwing tubes
and polishing lenses and adjusting reflectors, and
only after much labour the finely focussed instrument was brought to bear. Then he blew out the
light, and left the star to do its work upon the
plate alone. The day's task for the Christian is to
bring his instrument to bear. Having done that
he may blow out his candle. All the evidences of
Christianity which have brought him there, all
aids to Faith, all acts of Worship, all the leverages
of the Church, all Prayer and Meditation, all gird-
ing of the Will—these lesser processes, these
candle-light activities for that supreme hour may
be set aside. But, remember, it is but for an
hour. The wise man will be he who quickest lights
his candle; the wisest he who never let it out.
To-morrow, the next moment, he, a poor, darkened,
blurred soul, may need it again to focus the Image
better, to take a mote off the lens, to clear the
mirror from a breath with which the world has
dulled it.

No re-adjustment is ever required on behalf of
the Star. That is one great fixed point in this shifting

universe. But *the world moves*. And each day, each hour, demands a further motion and re-adjustment for the soul. A telescope in an observatory follows a star by clockwork, but the clockwork of the soul is called *the Will*. Hence, while the soul in passivity reflects the Image of the Lord, the Will in intense activity holds the mirror in position lest the drifting motion of the world bear it beyond the line of vision. To " follow Christ " is largely to keep the soul in such position as will allow for the motion of the earth. And this calculated counter-acting of the movements of a world, this holding of the mirror exactly opposite to the Mirrored, this steadying of the faculties unerringly, through cloud and earthquake, fire and sword, is the stupendous co-operating labour of the Will. It is all man's work. It is all Christ's work. In practice, it is both ; in theory it is both. But the wise man will say in practice, " It depends upon myself."

In the Galerie des Beaux Arts in Paris there stands a famous statue. It was the last work of a great genius, who, like many a genius, was very poor and lived in a garret, which served as studio and sleeping-room alike. When the statue was all but finished, one midnight a sudden frost fell upon Paris. The sculptor lay awake in the fireless room and thought of the still moist clay, thought how the water would freeze in the pores and destroy in an hour the dream of his life. So the old man rose from his couch and heaped the bed-clothes reverently round his work. In the morning when the neighbours entered the room the sculptor was dead. But the statue lived.

The Image of Christ that is forming within us —that is life's one charge. Let every project stand aside for that. " Till Christ be formed " no man's work is finished, no religion crowned, no life has fulfilled its end. Is the infinite task begun ? When, how, are we to be different ? Time cannot change men. Death cannot change men. Christ can. Wherefore, *put on Christ*.

V.

PAX VOBISCUM

Come unto Me all ye that are weary and heavy-laden And I will give you Rest

Take My Yoke upon you and learn of Me, for I am Meek and Lowly in heart, and ye shall find Rest unto your souls. For My Yoke is easy and My Burden light.

PAX VOBISCUM

I HEARD the other morning a sermon by a distinguished preacher upon " Rest." It was full of delightful thoughts ; but when I came to ask myself, " How does he say I can get Rest ? " there was no answer. The sermon was sincerely meant to be practical, yet it contained no experience that seemed to me to be tangible, nor any advice which could help me to find the thing itself as I went about the world that afternoon. Yet this omission of the only important problem was not the fault of the preacher. The whole popular religion is in the twilight here. And when pressed for really working specifics for the experiences with which it deals, it falters, and seems to lose itself in mist.

This want of connection between the great words of religion and every-day life has bewildered and discouraged all of us. Christianity possesses the noblest words in the language ; its literature overflows with terms expressive of the greatest and happiest moods which can fill the soul of man.

Rest, Joy, Peace, Faith, Love, Light—these words occur with such persistency in hymns and prayers that an observer might think they formed the staple of Christian experience. But on coming to close quarters with the actual life of most of us, how surely would he be disenchanted. I do not think we ourselves are aware how much our religious life is made up of phrases; how much of what we call Christian experience is only a dialect of the Churches, a mere religious phraseology with almost nothing behind it in what we really feel and know.

To some of us, indeed, the Christian experiences seem further away than when we took the first steps in the Christian life. That life has not opened out as we had hoped; we do not regret our religion, but we are disappointed with it. There are times, perhaps, when wandering notes from a diviner music stray into our spirits; but these experiences come at few and fitful moments. We have no sense of possession in them. When they visit us, it is a surprise. When they leave us, it is without explanation. When we wish their return, we do not know how to secure it.

All which points to a religion without solid base, and a poor and flickering life. It means a great bankruptcy in those experiences which give

Christianity its personal solace and make it attractive to the world, and a great uncertainty as to any remedy. It is as if we knew everything about health—except the way to get it.

I am quite sure that the difficulty does not lie in the fact that men are not in earnest. This is simply not the fact. All around us Christians are wearing themselves out in trying to be better. The amount of spiritual longing in the world— in the hearts of unnumbered thousands of men and women in whom we should never suspect it ; among the wise and thoughtful ; among the young and gay, who seldom assuage and never betray their thirst—this is one of the most wonderful and touching facts of life. It is not more heat that is needed, but more light ; not more force, but a wiser direction to be given to very real energies already there.

What Christian experience wants is *thread*, a vertebral column, method. It is impossible to believe that there is no remedy for its unevenness and dishevelment, or that the remedy is a secret. The idea, also, that some few men, by happy chance or happier temperament, have acquired the secret—as if there were some sort of knack or trick of it—is wholly incredible. Religion must ripen its fruit for men of every temperament ; and the

way even into its highest heights must be by a
gateway through which the peoples of the world
may pass.

I shall try to lead up to this gateway by a very
familiar path. But as that path is strangely un-
frequented, and even unknown where it passes
into the religious sphere, I must dwell for a moment
on the commonest of commonplaces.

EFFECTS REQUIRE CAUSES

NOTHING that happens in the world happens by
chance. God is a God of order. Everything is
arranged upon definite principles, and never at
random. The world, even the religious world, is
governed by law. Character is governed by law.
Happiness is governed by law. The Christian
experiences are governed by law. Men, forgetting
this, expect Rest, Joy, Peace, Faith, to drop into
their souls from the air like snow or rain. But in
point of fact they do not do so; and if they
did they would no less have their origin in previous
activities and be controlled by natural laws. Rain
and snow do drop from the air, but not without a
long previous history. They are the mature effects
of former causes. Equally so are Rest, and Peace,

and Joy. They, too, have each a previous history. Storms and winds and calms are not accidents, but are brought about by antecedent circumstances. Rest and Peace are but calms in man's inward nature, and arise through causes as definite and as inevitable.

Realise it thoroughly : it is a methodical not an accidental world. If a housewife turns out a good cake, it is the result of a sound receipt, carefully applied. She cannot mix the assigned ingredients and fire them for the appropriate time without producing the result. It is not she who has made the cake ; it is nature. She brings related things together ; sets causes at work ; these causes bring about the result. She is not a creator, but an intermediary. She does not expect random causes to produce specific effects—random ingredients would only produce random cakes. So it is in the making of Christian experiences. Certain lines are followed ; certain effects are the result. These effects cannot but be the result. But the result can never take place without the previous cause. To expect results without antecedents is to expect cakes without ingredients. That impossibility is precisely the almost universal expectation. Now what I mainly wish to do is to help you to firmly grasp this simple principle of Cause and

Effect in the spiritual world. And instead of applying the principle generally to each of the Christian experiences in turn, I shall examine its application to one in some little detail. The one I shall select is Rest. And I think anyone who follows the application in this single instance will be able to apply it for himself to all the others.

Take such a sentence as this : African explorers are subject to fevers which cause restlessness and delirium. Note the expression, " cause restlessness." *Restlessness has a cause.* Clearly, then, anyone who wished to get rid of restlessness would proceed at once to deal with the cause. If that were not removed, a doctor might prescribe a hundred things, and all might be taken in turn, without producing the least effect. Things are so arranged in the original planning of the world that certain effects must follow certain causes, and certain causes must be abolished before certain effects can be removed. Certain parts of Africa are inseparably linked with the physical experience called fever ; this fever is in turn infallibly linked with a mental experience called restlessness and delirium. To abolish the mental experience the radical method would be to abolish the physical experience, and the way of abolishing the physical experience would be to abolish Africa, or to cease to go there. Now this holds good for all other forms of Restlessness. Every other form and kind of Restlessness in the world has a definite cause, and the particular kind of Restlessness can only be removed by removing the allotted cause.

All this is also true of Rest. Restlessness has a cause : Must not *Rest* have a cause ? Necessarily. If it were a chance world we would not expect this ; but, being a methodical world, it cannot be otherwise. Rest, physical rest, moral rest, spiritual rest, every kind of rest has a cause, as certainly as restlessness. Now causes are discriminating. There is one kind of cause for every particular effect, and no other ; and if one particular effect is desired, the corresponding cause must be set in motion. It is no use proposing finely devised schemes, or going through general pious exercises in the hope that somehow Rest will come. The Christian life is not casual but causal. All nature is a standing protest against the absurdity of expecting to secure spiritual effects, or any effects, without the employment of appropriate causes. The Great Teacher dealt what ought to have been the final blow to this infinite irrelevancy by a single question, "Do men gather grapes of thorns or figs of thistles?"

Why, then, did the Great Teacher not educate His followers fully ? Why did He not tell us, for example, how such a thing as Rest might be obtained ? The answer is, that *He did*. But plainly, explicitly, in so many words ? Yes, plainly, explicitly, in so many words. He assigned Rest to its cause, in words with which each of us has been familiar from our earliest childhood.

He begins, you remember—for you at once know the passage I refer to—almost as if Rest could be had without any cause : " Come unto Me," He says, " and I will *give* you Rest."

Rest, apparently, was a favour to be bestowed ; men had but to come to Him ; He would give it to every applicant. But the next sentence takes that all back. The qualification, indeed, is added instantaneously. For what the first sentence seemed to give was next thing to an impossibility. For how, in a literal sense, can Rest be *given* ? One could no more give away Rest than he could give away Laughter. We speak of " causing " laughter, which we can do ; but we cannot give it away. When we speak of giving pain, we know perfectly well we cannot give pain away. And when we aim at giving pleasure, all that we do is to arrange a set of circumstances in such a way as that these shall cause pleasure. Of course there is a sense, and a very wonderful sense, in which a Great Personality breathes upon all who come within its influence an abiding peace and trust. Men can be to other men as the shadow of a great rock in a thirsty land. Much more Christ; much more Christ as Perfect Man; much more still as Saviour of the world. But it is not this of which I speak. When Christ said He would give men Rest, He meant simply that He would put them in the way of it. By no act of conveyance would, or could, He make over His own Rest to them. He could give them His receipt for it. That was all. But He would not make it for them; for one thing, it was not in His plan to make it for them; for another thing, men were not so planned that it could be made for them; and for yet another thing, it was a thousand times better that they should make it for themselves.

That this is the meaning becomes obvious from the wording of the second sentence: "Learn of Me and ye shall *find* Rest." Rest, that is to say, is not a thing that can be given, but a thing to be *acquired*. It comes not by an act, but by a process. It is not to be found in a happy hour, as one finds a treasure; but slowly, as one finds knowledge. It could indeed be no more found in a moment than could knowledge. A soil has to be prepared for it. Like a fine fruit, it will grow in one climate and not in another; at one altitude and not at another. Like all growths it will have an orderly development and mature by slow degrees.

The nature of this slow process Christ clearly defines when He says we are to achieve Rest by *learning*. "Learn of Me," He says, "and ye shall find rest to your souls." Now consider the extraordinary originality of this utterance. How novel the connection between these two words, "Learn" and "Rest"? How few of us have ever associated them—ever thought that Rest was a thing to be learned; ever laid ourselves out for it as we would to learn a language; ever practised it as we would practise the violin. Does it not show how entirely new Christ's teaching still is to the world, that so old and threadbare an aphorism should still be so little applied? The last thing most of us would have thought of would have been to associate *Rest* with *Work*.

What must one work at? What is that which if duly learned will find the soul of man in Rest? Christ answers without the least hesitation. He specifies two things—Meekness and Lowliness. "Learn of Me," He says, "for I am *meek* and *lowly* in heart." Now these two things are not chosen at random. To these accomplishments, in a special way, Rest is attached. Learn these, in short, and you have already found Rest. These as they stand are direct causes of Rest ; will produce it at once ; cannot but produce it at once. And if you think for a single moment, you will see how this is necessarily so, for causes are never arbitrary, and the connection between antecedent and consequent here and everywhere lies deep in the nature of things.

What is the connection, then ? I answer by a further question. What are the chief causes of *Unrest* ? If you know yourself, you will answer Pride, Selfishness, Ambition. As you look back upon the past years of your life, is it not true that its unhappiness has chiefly come from the succession of personal mortifications and almost trivial disappointments which the intercourse of life has brought you ? Great trials come at lengthened intervals, and we rise to breast them ; but it is the petty friction of our every-day life with one another, the jar of business or of work, the discord of the domestic circle, the collapse of our ambition, the crossing of our will, the taking down of our conceit, which make inward peace impossible. Wounded vanity, then, disappointed hopes, unsatisfied selfishness—these are the old, vulgar, universal sources of man's unrest.

Now it is obvious why Christ pointed out as the two chief objects for attainment the exact opposites of these. To Meekness and Lowliness these things simply do not exist. They cure unrest by making it impossible. These remedies do not trifle with surface symptoms ; they strike at once at removing causes. The ceaseless chagrin of a self-centered life can be removed at once by learning Meekness and Lowliness of heart. He who learns them is for ever proof against it. He lives henceforth a charmed life. Christianity is a fine inoculation, a transfusion of healthy blood into an anæmic or poisoned soul. No fever can attack a perfectly sound body ; no fever of unrest can disturb a soul which has breathed the air or learned the ways of Christ. Men sigh for the wings of a dove that they may fly away and be at Rest. But flying away will not help us. " The Kingdom of God is *within you*." We aspire to the top to look for Rest ; it lies at the bottom. Water rests only when it gets to the lowest place. So do men. Hence, be lowly. The man who has no opinion of himself at all can never be hurt if others do not acknowledge him. Hence, be meek. He who is without expectation cannot fret if nothing comes to him. It is self-evident that these things are so. The lowly man and the meek man are really above all other men, above all other things. They dominate the world because they do not care for it. The miser does not possess gold, gold possesses him. But the meek possess it. " The meek," said Christ, " inherit the earth." They do not buy it ; they do not conquer it ; but they inherit it.

There are people who go about the world looking out for slights, and they are necessarily miserable, for they find them at every turn—especially the imaginary ones. One has the same pity for such men as for the very poor. They are the morally illiterate. They have had no real education, for they have never learned how to live. Few men know how to live. We grow up at random, carrying into mature life the merely animal methods and motives which we had as little children. And it does not occur to us that all this must be changed ; that much of it must be reversed ; that life is the finest of the Fine Arts ; that it has to be learned with lifelong patience, and that the years of our pilgrimage are all too short to master it triumphantly.

Yet this is what Christianity is for—to teach men the Art of Life. And its whole curriculum lies in one word—" Learn of Me." Unlike most education, this is almost purely personal; it is not to be had from books or lectures or creeds or doctrines. It is a study from the life. Christ never said much in mere words about the Christian graces. He lived them, He was them. Yet we do not merely copy Him. We learn His art by living with Him, like the old apprentices with their masters.

Now we understand it all? Christ's invitation to the weary and heavy-laden is a call to begin life over again upon a new principle—upon His own principle. "Watch My way of doing things," He says. "Follow Me. Take life as I take it. Be meek and lowly and you will find Rest."

I do not say, remember, that the Christian life to every man, or to any man, can be a bed of roses. No educational process can be this. And perhaps if some men knew how much was involved in the simple "learn" of Christ, they would not enter His school with so irresponsible a heart. For there is not only much to learn, but much to un-learn. Many men never go to this school at all till their disposition is already half ruined and character has taken on its fatal set. To learn arith-metic is difficult at fifty—much more to learn Christianity. To learn simply what it is to be meek and lowly, in the case of one who has had no lessons in that in childhood, may cost him half of what he values most on earth. Do we realise, for instance, that the way of teaching humility is generally by *humiliation*? There is probably no other school for it. When a man enters himself as a pupil in such a school it means a very great thing. There is much Rest there, but there is also much Work.

I should be wrong, even though my theme is the brighter side, to ignore the cross and minimise the cost. Only it gives to the cross a more definite meaning, and a rarer value, to connect it thus directly and *causally* with the growth of the inner life. Our platitudes on the " benefits of affliction " are usually about as vague as our theories of Christian Experience. " Somehow," we believe affliction does us good. But it is not a question of " Somehow." The result is definite, calculable, necessary. It is under the strictest law of cause and effect. The first effect of losing one's fortune, for instance, is humiliation ; and the effect of humiliation, as we have just seen, is to make one humble ; and the effect of being humble is to produce Rest. It is a round-about way, apparently, of producing Rest ; but Nature generally works by circular processes ; and it is not certain that there is any other way of becoming humble, or of finding Rest. If a man could make himself humble to order, it might simplify matters, but we do not find that this happens. Hence we must all go through the mill. Hence death, death to the lower self, is the nearest gate, and the quickest road to life.

Yet this is only half the truth. Christ's life outwardly was one of the most troubled lives that was ever lived : Tempest and tumult, tumult and tempest, the waves breaking over it all the time till the worn body was laid in the grave. But the inner life was a sea of glass. The great calm was always there. At any moment you might have gone to Him and found Rest. And even when the blood-hounds were dogging Him in the streets of Jerusalem, He turned to His disciples and offered them, as a last legacy, " My peace." Nothing ever for a moment broke the serenity of Christ's life on earth. Misfortune could not reach him ; He had no fortune. Food, raiment, money—fountain-heads of half the world's weariness—He simply did not care for ; they played no part in His life ; He " took no thought " for them. It was impossible to affect Him by lowering His reputation ; He had already made Himself of no reputation. He was dumb before insult. When He was reviled He reviled not again. In fact, there was nothing that the world could do to Him that could ruffle the surface of His spirit.

Such living, as mere living, is altogether unique. It is only when we see what it was in Him that we can know what the word Rest means. It lies not in emotions, nor in the absence of emotions. It is not a hallowed feeling that comes over us in church. It is not something that the preacher has in his voice. It is not in nature, nor in poetry, nor in music—though in all these there is soothing. It is the mind at leisure from itself. It is the perfect poise of the soul ; the absolute adjustment of the inward man to the stress of all outward things ; the preparedness against every emergency ; the stability of assured convictions ; the eternal calm of an invulnerable faith ; the repose of a heart set deep in God. It is the mood of the man who says, with Browning, " God's in His Heaven, all's well with the world."

Two painters each painted a picture to illustrate his conception of rest. The first chose for his scene a still, lone lake among the far-off mountains. The second threw on his canvas a thundering water-fall, with a fragile birch-tree bending over the foam ; at the fork of a branch, almost wet with the cataract's spray, a robin sat on its nest. The first was only *Stagnation ;* the last was *Rest.* For in Rest there are always two elements—tranquillity and energy ; silence and turbulence ; creation and destruction ; fearlessness and fearfulness. This it was in Christ.

It is quite plain from all this that whatever else He claimed to be or to do, He at least knew how to live. All this is the perfection of living, of living in the mere sense of passing through the world in the best way. Hence His anxiety to communicate His idea of life to others. He came, He said, to give men life, true life, a more abundant life than they were living ; " the life," as the fine phrase in the Revised Version has it, " that is life indeed." This is what He himself possessed, and it was this which He offers to all mankind. And hence His direct appeal for all to come to Him who had not made much of life, who were weary and heavy-laden. These He would teach His secret. They, also, should know " the life that is life indeed."

WHAT YOKES ARE FOR

THERE is still one doubt to clear up. After the statement, " Learn of Me," Christ throws in the disconcerting qualification, " *Take My yoke* upon you and learn of Me." Why, if all this be true, does He call it a *yoke* ? Why, while professing to give Rest, does He with the next breath whisper " *burden* " ? Is the Christian life after all, what its enemies take it for—an additional weight to the already great woe of life, some extra punctiliousness about duty, some painful devotion to observances, some heavy restriction and trammelling of all that is joyous and free in the world ? Is life not hard and sorrowful enough without being fettered with yet another yoke ?

It is astounding how so glaring a misunderstanding of this plain sentence should ever have passed into currency. Did you ever stop to ask what a yoke is really for ? Is it to be a burden to the animal which wears it ? It is just the opposite. It is to make its burden light. Attached to the oxen in any other way than by a yoke, the plough would be intolerable. Worked by means of a yoke, it is light. A yoke is not an instrument of torture ; it is an instrument of mercy. It is not a malicious contrivance for making work hard ; it is a gentle device to make hard labour light. It is not meant to give pain, but to save pain. And yet men speak of the yoke of Christ as if it were a slavery, and look upon those who wear it as objects of compassion ? For generations we have had homilies on " The Yoke of Christ," some delighting in portraying its narrow exactions ; some seeking in these exactions the marks of its divinity ; others apologising for it, and toning it down ; still others assuring us that, although it be very bad, it is not to be compared with the positive blessings of

Christianity. How many, especially among the young, has this one mistaken phrase driven for ever away from the kingdom of God? Instead of making Christ attractive, it makes Him out a task-master, narrowing life by petty restrictions, calling for self-denial where none is necessary, making misery a virtue under the plea that it is the yoke of Christ, and happiness criminal because it now and then evades is. According to this conception, Christians are at best the victims of a depressing fate ; their life is a penance ; and their hope for the next world purchased by a slow martyrdom in this.

The mistake has arisen from taking the word " yoke " here in the same sense as in the expressions " under the yoke," or " wear the yoke in his youth." But in Christ's illustration it is not the *jugum* of the Roman soldier, but the simple " harness " or " ox-collar " of the Eastern peasant. It is the literal wooden yoke which He, with His own hands in the carpenter's shop, had probably often made. He knew the difference between a smooth yoke and a rough one, a bad fit and a good fit ; the difference also it made to the patient animal which had to wear it. The rough yoke galled, and the burden was heavy ; the smooth yoke caused no pain, and the load was lightly drawn. The badly fitted

harness was a misery ; the well fitted collar was
" easy."

And what was the " burden " ? It was not some
special burden laid upon the Christian, some unique
infliction that he alone must bear. It was what all
men bear. It was simply life, human life itself,
the general burden of life which all must carry with
them from the cradle to the grave. Christ saw that
men took life painfully. To some it was a weariness,
to others a failure, to many a tragedy, to all a
struggle and a pain. How to carry this burden of
life had been the whole world's problem. It is
still the whole world's problem. And here is
Christ's solution : " Carry it as I do. Take life
as I take it. Look at it from My point of view.
Interpret it upon My principles. Take My yoke
and learn of Me, and you will find it easy. For My
yoke is easy, works easily, sits right upon the
shoulders, and *therefore* My burden is light."

There is no suggestion here that religion will
absolve any man from bearing burdens. That would
be to absolve him from living, since it is life itself
that is the burden. What Christianity does propose
is to make it tolerable. Christ's yoke is simply
His secret for the alleviation of human life, His
prescription for the best and happiest method of
living. Men harness themselves to the work and

stress of the world in clumsy and unnatural ways.
The harness they put on is antiquated. A rough,
ill-fitted collar at the best, they make its strain
and friction past enduring, by placing it where
the neck is most sensitive ; and by mere continuous
irritation this sensitiveness increases until the
whole nature is quick and sore.

This is the origin, among other things, of a
disease called "touchiness"—a disease which,
in spite of its innocent name, is one of the gravest
sources of restlessness in the world. Touchiness,
when it becomes chronic, is a morbid condition of the
inward disposition. It is self-love inflamed to the
acute point ; conceit, *with a hair-trigger*. The cure
is to shift the yoke to some other place ; to let men
and things touch us through some new and perhaps
as yet unused part of our nature ; to become meek
and lowly in heart while the old nature is becoming
numb from want of use. It is the beautiful work of
Christianity everywhere to adjust the burden of
life to those who bear it, and them to it. It has a
perfectly miraculous gift of healing. Without
doing any violence to human nature it sets it right
with life, harmonising it with all surrounding things,
and restoring those who are jaded with the fatigue
and dust of the world to a new grace of living. In
the mere matter of altering the perspective of life

and changing the proportions of things, its function in lightening the care of man is altogether its own. The weight of a load depends upon the attraction of the earth. But suppose the attraction of the earth were removed ? A ton on some other planet, where the attraction of gravity is less, does not weigh half a ton. Now Christianity removes the attraction of the earth, and this is one way in which it diminishes men's burden. It makes them citizens of another world. What was a ton yesterday is not half a ton to-day. So, without changing one's circumstances, merely by offering a wider horizon and a different standard, it alters the whole aspect of the world.

Christianity as Christ taught it is the truest philosophy of life ever spoken. But let us be quite sure when we speak of Christianity that we mean Christ's Christianity. Other versions are either caricatures, or exaggerations, or misunderstandings, or short-sighted and surface readings. For the most part their attainment is hopeless and the results wretched. But I care not who the person is, or through what vale of tears he has passed, or is about to pass, there is a new life for him along this path.

HOW FRUITS GROW

WERE Rest my subject, there are other things I should wish to say about it, and other kinds of Rest of which I should like to speak. But that is not my subject. My theme is that the Christian experiences are not the work of magic, but come under the law of Cause and Effect. And I have chosen Rest only as a single illustration of the working of that principle. If there were time I might next run over all the Christian experiences in turn, and show how the same wide law applies to each. But I think it may serve the better purpose if I leave this further exercise to yourselves. I know no Bible study that you will find more full of fruit, or which will take you nearer to the ways of God, or make the Christian life itself more solid or more sure. I shall add only a single other illustration of what I mean, before I close.

Where does Joy come from ? I knew a Sunday scholar whose conception of Joy was that it was a thing made in lumps and kept somewhere in Heaven, and that when people prayed for it, pieces were somehow let down and fitted into their souls. I am not sure that views as gross and material are not often held by people who ought to be

wiser. In reality, Joy is as much a matter of
Cause and Effect as pain. No one can get Joy by
merely asking for it. It is one of the ripest fruits
of the Christian life, and, like all fruits, must be
grown. There is a very clever trick in India called
the mango-trick. A seed is put in the ground and
covered up, and after divers incantations a full-
blown mango-bush appears within five minutes.
I never met anyone who knew how the thing was
done, but I never met anyone who believed it to
be anything else than a conjuring-trick. The world
is pretty unanimous now in its belief in the orderli-
ness of Nature. Men may not know how fruits
grow, but they do know that they cannot grow in
five minutes. Some lives have not even a stalk on
which fruits could hang, even if they did grow in
five minutes. Some have never planted one sound
seed of Joy in all their lives ; and others who may
have planted a germ or two have lived so little in
sunshine that they never could come to maturity.

Whence, then, is Joy ? Christ put His teaching
upon this subject into one of the most exquisite
of His parables. I should in any instance have
appealed to His teaching here, as in the case of
Rest, for I do not wish you to think I am speaking
words of my own. But it so happens that He has
dealt with it in a passage of unusual fulness.

I need not recall the whole illustration. It is the parable of the Vine. Did you ever think why Christ spoke that parable? He did not merely throw it into space as a fine illustration of general truths. It was not simply a statement of the mystical union, and the doctrine of an indwelling Christ. It was that; but it was more. After He had said it, He did what was not an unusual thing when He was teaching His greatest lessons. He turned to the disciples and said He would tell them why He had spoken it. It was to tell them how to get Joy. "These things have I spoken unto you," He said, "that My joy might remain in you and that your Joy might be full." It was a purposed and deliberate communication of His secret of Happiness.

Go back over these verses, then, and you will find the Causes of this Effect, the spring, and the only spring, out of which true Happiness comes. I am not going to analyse them in detail. I ask you to enter into the words for yourselves. Remember, in the first place, that the Vine was the Eastern symbol of Joy. It was its fruit that made glad the heart of man. Yet, however innocent that gladness—for the expressed juice of the grape was the common drink at every peasant's board—the gladness was only a gross and passing thing. This was not true happiness, and the vine of the Palestine vineyards was not the true vine. *Christ* was " the *true* Vine." Here, then, is the ultimate source of Joy. Through whatever media it reaches us, all true Joy and Gladness find their source in Christ. By this, of course, is not meant that the actual Joy experienced is transferred from Christ's nature, or is something passed on from Him to us. What is passed on is His method of getting it. There is, indeed, a sense in which we can share another's joy or another's sorrow. But that is another matter. Christ is the source of Joy to men in the sense in which He is the source of rest. His people share His life, and therefore share its consequences, and one of these is Joy. His method of living is one that in the nature of things produces Joy. When He spoke of His Joy remaining with us He meant in part that the causes which produced it should continue to act. His followers, that is to say, by *repeating* His life would experience its accompaniments. His Joy, His kind of Joy, would remain with them.

The medium through which this Joy comes is next explained : " He that abideth in Me the same bringeth forth much fruit." Fruit first, Joy next ; the one the cause or medium of the other. Fruit-bearing is the necessary antecedent ; Joy both the necessary consequent and the necessary accompaniment. It lies partly in the bearing fruit, partly in the fellowship which makes that possible. Partly that is to say, Joy lies in mere constant living in Christ's presence, with all that that implies of peace, of shelter, and of love ; partly in the influence of that Life upon mind and character and will ; and partly in the inspiration to live and work for others, with all that that brings of self-riddance and Joy in other's gain. All these, in different ways and at different times, are sources of pure Happiness. Even the simplest of them —to do good to other people—is an instant and infallible specific. There is no mystery about Happiness whatever. Put in the right ingredients and it must come out. He that abideth in Him will bring forth much fruit ; and bringing forth much fruit is Happiness. The infallible receipt for Happiness, then, is to do good ; and the infallible receipt for doing good is to abide in Christ. The surest proof that all this is a plain matter of Cause and Effect is that men may try every other conceivable way of finding Happiness, and they will fail. Only the right cause in each case can produce the right effect.

Then the Christian experiences are our own making ? In the same sense in which grapes are

our own making, and no more. All fruits *grow*—
whether they grow in the soil or in the soul ;
whether they are the fruits of the wild grape or of
the True Vine. No man can *make* things grow. He
can *get them to grow* by arranging all the circumstances and fulfilling all the conditions. But the
growing is done by God. Causes and effects are
eternal arrangements, set in the constitution of the
world ; fixed beyond man's ordering. What man
can do is to place himself in the midst of a chain
of sequences. Thus he can get things to grow :
thus he himself can grow. But the grower is the
Spirit of God.

What more need I add but this—test the method
by experiment. Do not imagine that you have got
these things because you know how to get them.
As well try to feed upon a cookery book. But I
think I can promise that if you try in this simple
and natural way, you will not fail. Spend the time
you have spent in sighing for fruits in fulfilling
the conditions of their growth. The fruits will
come, must come. We have hitherto paid immense
attention to *effects*, to the mere experiences themselves ; we have described them, extolled them,
advised them, prayed for them—done everything
but find out what *caused* them. Henceforth let
us deal with causes. " To be," says Lotze, " is to be

in relations." About every other method of living
the Christian life there is an uncertainty. About
every other method of acquiring the Christian
experiences there is a " perhaps." But in so far
as this method is the way of nature, it cannot fail.
Its guarantee is the laws of the universe, and these
are " the Hands of the Living God."

PART TWO
THE WILL OF GOD

With the exception of No. II., now printed for the first time, these addresses are from "The Ideal Life," published in 1897.

I.

THE MAN AFTER
GOD'S OWN HEART

THE MAN AFTER GOD'S OWN HEART

A BIBLE STUDY ON THE IDEAL OF A CHRISTIAN LIFE

" A man after mine own heart, who shall fulfil
all my will."—ACTS xiii. 22

No man can be making much of his life who has
not a very definite conception of what he is living
for. And if you ask, at random, a dozen men what
is the end of their life, you will be surprised to
find how few have formed to themselves more than
the most dim idea. The question of the *summum
bonum* has ever been the most difficult for the
human mind to grasp. What shall a man do with
his life ? What is life for ? Why is it given ? These
have been the one great puzzle for human books
and human brains ; and ancient philosophy and
mediæval learning and modern culture alike have
failed to tell us what these mean.

No man, no book save one, has ever told the
world what it wants ; so each has had to face the
problem in his own uncertain light, and carry out,
each for himself, the life that he thinks best.

Here is one who says literature is the great thing—he will be a literary man. He lays down for himself his ideal of a literary life. He surrounds himself with the best ideals of style ; and with his great ambition working towards great ends, after great models, he cuts out for himself what he thinks is his great life work. Another says the world is the great thing—he will be a man of the world. A third will be a business man ; a fourth, a man of science. And each follows out his aim.

And the Christian must have a definite aim and model for his life. These aims are great aims, but not great enough for him. His one book has taught him a nobler life than all the libraries of the rich and immortal past. He may wish to be a man of business, or a man of science, and indeed he may be both. But he covets a nobler name than these. He will be the man after God's own heart. He has found out the secret philosophy never knew, that the ideal life is this—" A man after Mine own heart, who shall fulfil all My will." And just as the man of the world, or the literary man, lays down a programme for the brief span of his working life, which he feels must vanish shortly in the Unknown of the grave, so much more will the Christian for the great span of his life before it arches over into eternity.

He is a great man who has a great plan for his
life—the greatest who has the greatest plan and
keeps it. And the Christian should have the
greatest plan, as his life is the greatest, as his
work is the greatest, as his life and his work will
follow him when all this world's is done.

Now we are going to ask to-day, What is the
true plan of the Christian life? We shall need a
definition that we may know it, a description that
we may follow it. And if you look, you will see
that both, in a sense, lie on the surface of our text.
" A man after Mine own heart,"—here is the
definition of what we are to be. " Who shall fulfil
all My will,"—here is the description of how we
are to be it. These words are the definition and
the description of the model human life. They
describe the man after God's own heart. They
give us the key to the Ideal Life.

The general truth of these words is simply this :
that the end of life is to do God's will. Now that
is a great and surprising revelation. No man ever
found that out. It has been before the world these
eighteen hundred years, yet few have even found
it out to-day. One will tell you the end of life is
to be true. Another will tell you it is to deny self.
Another will say it is to keep the Ten Commandments. A fourth will point you to the Beatitudes.

One will tell you it is to *do* good, another that it is to *get* good, another that it is to *be* good. But the end of life is in none of these things. It is more than all, and it includes them all. The end of life is not to deny self, nor to be true, nor to keep the Ten Commandments—it is simply to do God's will. It is not to get good, nor be good, nor even to do good—it is just what God wills, whether that be working or waiting, or winning, or losing, or suffering, or recovering, or living, or dying.

But this conception is too great for us. It is not practical enough. It is the greatest conception of man that has ever been given to the world. The great philosophers, from Socrates and Plato to Immanuel Kant and Mill, have given us their conception of an ideal human life. But none of them is at all so great as this. Each of them has constructed an ideal human life, a universal life they call it, a life for all other lives, a life for all men and all time to copy. None of them is half so deep, so wonderful, so far-reaching, as this : " A man after Mine own heart, who shall fulfil all My will."

But exactly for this very reason it is at first sight impracticable. We feel helpless beside a truth so great and eternal. God must teach us these things. Like little children, we must sit at

His feet and learn. And as we come to Him with
our difficulty, we find He has prepared two practical helps for us, that He may humanise the lesson
and bring it near to us, so that by studying these
helps, and following them with willing and humble
hearts, we shall learn to copy into our lives the
great ideal of God.

The two helps which God has given us are these :

I. The Model Life realised in Christ, the living
Word.

II. The Model Life analysed in the Bible, the
written Word.

The usual method is to deal almost exclusively
with the first of these. To-day, for certain reasons,
we mean to consider the second. As regards the
first, of course, if a man could follow Christ he
would lead the model life. But what is meant by
telling a man to follow Christ ? How is it to be
done ? It is like putting a young artist before a
Murillo or a Raphael, and telling him to copy it.
But even as the artist in following his ideal has
colours put into his hand, and brush and canvas,
and a hint here from his master, and a touch
there from another, so with the pupil in the school
of Christ. The great Master Himself is there to
help him. The Holy Spirit is there to help him.
But the model of life is not to be mystically

attained. There is spirituality about it, but no unreality. So God has provided another great help, our second help : The Model Life analysed in the Word of God. Without the one, the ideal life would be incredible ; without the other, it would be unintelligible. Hence God has given us two sides of this model life : realised in the Living Word ; analysed in the written Word.

Let us search our Bibles then to find this ideal life, so that copying it in our lives, reproducing it day by day and point by point, we may learn to make the most of our life, and have it said of us, as it was of David, " A man after Mine own heart, who shall fulfil all My will."

(1) The first thing our ideal man wants is a reason for his being alive at all. He must account for his existence. What is he here for ? And the Bible answer is this : " I come to do Thy will, O God " (Heb. x. 7).

That is what we are here for—to do God's will. " I come to do Thy will, O God." That is the object of your life and mine—to do God's will. It is not to be happy or to be successful, or famous, or to do the best we can, and get on honestly in the world. It is something far higher than this— to do God's will. There, at the very outset, is the great key to life. Anyone of us can tell in a moment

whether our lives are right or not. Are we doing
God's will ? We do not mean, Are we doing God's
work ?—preaching or teaching, or collecting money
—but God's *will*. A man may think he is doing
God's work, when he is not even doing God's will.
And a man may be doing God's work and God's
will quite as much by hewing stones or sweeping
streets, as by preaching or praying. So the question
just means this—Are we working out our common
every-day life on the great lines of God's will ?
This is different from the world's model life. " I
come to push my way." This is the world's idea
of it. " Not my way, not my will, but Thine be
done "—this is the Christian's. This is what the
man after God's own heart says : " I seek not
mine own will, but the will of Him that sent
me."

(2) The second thing the ideal man needs is
Sustenance. After he has got life, you must give him
food. Now, what food shall you give him ? Shall
you feed him with knowledge, or with riches, or
with honour, or with beauty, or with power, or
truth ? No ; there is a rarer luxury than these—
so rare, that few have ever more than tasted it ; so
rich, that they who have will never live on other
fare again. It is this : " My meat is to do the will
of Him that sent Me " (John iv. 34).

Again, to do God's will. That is what a man lives for : it is also what he lives on. *Meat.* Meat is strength, support, nourishment. The strength of the model life is drawn from the Divine will. Man has a strong will. But God's will is everlasting strength—Almighty strength. Such strength the ideal man gets. He grows by it, he assimilates it—it is his life. " Man shall not live by bread alone, but by every word that cometh out of God." Nothing can satisfy his appetite but this. He hungers to do God's will. Nothing else will fill him. Every one knows that the world is hungry. But the hungry world is starving. It has many meats and many drinks, but there is no nourishment in them. It has pleasures, and gaiety, and excitement ; but there is no food there for the immortal craving of the soul. It has the theatre and worldly society, and worldly books, and worldly lusts. But these things merely intoxicate. There is no sustenance in them. So our ideal life turns its eye from them all with unutterable loathing. " *My* meat is to do God's will." To do God's will ! No possibility of starving on such wonderful fare as this. God's will is eternal. It is eternal food the Christian lives upon. In spring-time it is not sown, and in summer drought it cannot fail. In harvest it is not reaped, yet the storehouse is ever full. Oh, what possibilities of life it opens up! What possibilities of growth! What possibilities of work! How a soul develops on God's will!

(3) The next thing the ideal man needs is *Society*. Man is not made to be alone. He needs friendships. Without society, the ideal man would be a monster, a contradiction. You must give him friendship. Now, whom will you give him? Will you compliment him by calling upon the great men of the earth to come and minister to him? No. The ideal man does not want compliments. He has better food. Will you invite the ministers and the elders of the Church to meet him? Will you offer him the companionship of saint or angel, or seraphim or cherubim, as he treads his path through the wilderness of life? No; for none of these will satisfy him. He has a better friendship than saint or angel or seraphim or cherubim. The answer trembles on the lip of every one who is trying to follow the ideal life : " *Whosoever shall do the will of My Father which is in Heaven, the same is My brother, and sister, and mother* " (Matt. xii. 50 ; Mark iii. 35).

Yes. *My* brother, and *My* sister, and *My* mother. Mother! The path of life is dark and cheerless to you. There is a smoother path just by the side of it—a forbidden path. You have been tempted many a time to take it. But you knew it was wrong, and you paused. Then, with a sigh, you struck along the old weary path again. It was the will of God, you said. Brave mother ! Oh, if you knew it, there was a voice at your ear just then, as Jesus saw the brave thing you had done, " *My* mother ! " " He that doeth the will of My Father, the same is *My* mother." Yes ; this is the consolation of Christ—" My mother." What society to be in ! What about the darkness of the path, if we have the brightness of His smile ? Oh ! it is better, as the hymnist says :

" It is better to walk in the dark with God,
    Than walk alone in the light ;
It is better to walk with Him by faith,
    Than walk alone by sight."

Some young man here is suffering fierce temptation. To-day he feels strong ; but to-morrow his Sabbath resolutions will desert him. What will his companions say, if he does not join them ? He cannot face them if he is to play the Christian. Companions ! What are all the companions in the world to this ? What are all the friendships, the truest and the best, to this dear and sacred brotherhood of Christ ? " He that doeth the will of My Father, the same is *My* brother."

My mother, my brother, and my sister. He has a sister—some sister here. Sister! Your life is a quiet and even round of common and homely things. You dream, perhaps, of a wider sphere, and sigh for a great and useful life, like some women whose names you know. You question whether it is right that life should be such a little bundle of very little things. But nothing is little that is done for God, and it must be right if it be His will. And if this common life, with its homely things, is God's discipline for you, be assured that in your small corner, your unobserved, unambitious, simple woman's lot is very near and very dear to Him Who said, "Whosoever doeth the will of My Father, the same is My sister."

(4) Now we have found the ideal man a Friend. But he wants something more. He wants *Language*. He must speak to his Friend. He cannot be silent in such company. And speaking to such a Friend is not mere conversation. It has a higher name. It is communion. It is prayer. Well, we listen to hear the ideal man's prayer. Something about God's will it must be; for that is what he is sure to talk about. That is the object of His life. That is his meat. In that he finds his society. So he will be sure to talk about it. Every one knows what his prayer will be. Every one remembers the words

of the ideal prayer : " *Thy will be done* " (Matt. vi. 10).

Now mark the emphasis on *done*. He prays that God's will may be done. It is not that God's will may be borne, endured, put up with. There is activity in his prayer. It is not mere resignation. How often is this prayer toned off into mere endurance, sufferance, passivity. " Thy will be done," people say resignedly. " There is no help for it. We may just as well submit. God evidently means to have His way. Better to give in at once and make the best of it." Well, this is far from the ideal prayer. It may be nobler to suffer God's will than to do it ; perhaps it is. But there is nothing noble in resignation of this sort—this resignation under protest as it were. And it disguises the meaning of the prayer, " Thy will be done." It is intensely active. It is not an acquiescence simply in God's dealing. It is a cry for more of God's dealing—God's dealing with me, with everything, with everybody, with the whole world. It is an appeal to the mightiest energy in heaven or earth to work, to make more room for itself, to energise. It is a prayer that the Almighty energies of the Divine will may be universally known, and felt, and worshipped.

Now the ideal man has no deeper prayer than

that. He wants to get into the great current of Will, which flows silently out of Eternity, and swiftly back to Eternity again. His only chance of happiness, of usefulness, of work, is to join the living rill of his will to that. Other Christians miss it, or settle on the banks of the great stream ; but he will be among the forces and energies and powers, that he may link his weakness with God's greatness, and his simplicity with God's majesty, that he may become a force, an energy, a power for Duty and God. Perhaps God may do something with him. Certainly God will do something in him—for it is God who worketh in him both to will and to do of His good pleasure. So his one concern is to be kept in the will of God.

The ideal man has no deeper prayer than that. It is the truest language of his heart. He does not want a bed of roses, or his pathway strewn with flowers. He wants to do God's will. He does not want health or wealth, nor does he covet sickness or poverty,—just what God sends. He does not want success—even success in winning souls—or want of success. What God wills for him, that is all. He does not want to prosper in business, or to keep barely struggling on. God knows what is best. He does not want his friends to live, himself to live or die. God's will be done. The currents of his life flow far below the circumstances of things. There is a deeper principle in it than to live to gratify himself. And so he simply asks, that in the ordinary round of his daily life there may be no desire of his heart more deep, more vivid, more absorbingly present than this, " Thy will be done." He who makes this the prayer of his life will know that of all prayer it is the most truly blessed, the most nearly in the spirit of Him who sought not His own will, but the will of Him that sent Him.

" Lord Jesus, as Thou wilt ! if among thorns I go
   Still sometimes here and there let a few roses
     blow.
  No ! Thou on earth along the thorny path hast
     gone,
  Then lead me after Thee, my Lord ; Thy will be
     done."   *Schmolk.*

(5) But the ideal man does not always pray. There is such perfect blessedness in praying the ideal prayer that language fails him sometimes. The peace of God passes all understanding, much more all expression. It comes down upon the soul, and makes it ring with unutterable joy. And language stops. The ideal man can no longer

pray to his Friend. So his prayer changes into
Praise. He is too full to speak, so his heart bursts
into song. Therefore we must find in the Bible
the praise of his lips. And who does not remember
in the Psalms the song of the ideal man ? The
huntsmen would gather at night to sing of their
prowess in the chase, the shepherd would chant
the story of the lion or the bear which he killed as
he watched his flocks. But David takes down his
harp and sings a sweeter psalm than all : " *Thy
Statutes have been my Songs in the House of my
pilgrimage* " (Ps. cxix. 54). He knows no sweeter
strain. How different from those who think God's
law is a stern, cold thing ! God's law is His written
will. It has no terrors to the ideal man. He is
not afraid to think of its sternness and majesty.
" I will meditate on Thy laws day and night," he
says. He tells us the subject of his thoughts. Ask
him what he is thinking about at any time. " Thy
laws," he says. How he can please his Master,
what more he can bear for Him, what next he can
do for Him—he has no other pleasure in life than
this. You need not speak to him of the delights of
life. " I will delight myself in Thy statutes," he
says. You see what amusements the ideal man has.
You see where the sources of his enjoyment are.
Praise is the overflow of a full heart. When it is

full of enjoyment it overflows ; and you can tell the kind of enjoyment from the kind of praise that runs over. The ideal man's praise is of the will of God. He has no other sources of enjoyment. The cup of the world's pleasure has no attraction for him. The delights of life are bitter. Here is his only joy, his only delight : " I delight to do Thy will, O my God " (Ps. xl. 8).

(6) The next thing the ideal man wants is *Education*. He needs teaching. He must take his place with the other disciples at his Master's feet. What does he want from the great Teacher ? Teach me Wisdom ? No. Wisdom is not enough. Teach me what is Truth ? No, not even that. Teach me how to do good, how to love, how to trust ? No, there is a deeper want than all. " *Teach me to do Thy will* " (Ps. cxliii. 10). This is the true education. Teach me to do Thy will. This was the education of Christ. Wisdom is a great study, and truth, and good works, and love, and trust, but there is an earlier lesson—obedience. So the ideal pupil prays, " Teach me to do Thy will."

And now we have almost gone far enough. These are really all the things the ideal man can need. But in case he should want anything else, God has given the man after his own heart a promise. God never leaves anything unprovided for. An emergency might arise in the ideal man's life ; or he might make a mistake or lose heart, or be afraid to ask his Friend for some very great thing he needed, thinking it was too much, or for some very little thing, thinking it unworthy of notice. So God has given :

(7) The ideal *Promise :* " If we ask anything according to His will, He heareth us . . . and we know that we have the petitions that we desired from Him " (1 John v. 14). If he ask anything— no exception—no limit to God's confidence in him. He trusts him to ask right things. He is guiding him, even in what he asks, if he is the man after God's own heart ; so God sets no limit to his power. If anyone is doing God's will let him ask anything. It is God's will that he ask anything. Let him put His promise to the test.

Notice here what the true basis of prayer is. The prayer that is answered is the prayer after God's will. And the reason for this is plain. What is God's will is God's wish. And when a man does what God wills, he does what God wishes done. Therefore God will have that done at any cost, at any sacrifice. Thousands of prayers are never answered, simply because God does not wish them. If we pray for any one thing, or any number of things we are sure God wishes, we may be sure our wishes will be gratified. For our wishes are only the reflection of God's. And the wish in us is almost equivalent to the answer. It is the answer casting its shadow backwards. Already the thing is done in the mind of God. It casts two shadows—one backward, one forward. The backward shadow —that is the wish before the thing is done, which sheds itself in prayer. The forward shadow—that is the joy after the thing is done, which sheds itself in praise. Oh, what a rich and wonderful life this ideal life must be ! Asking anything, getting everything, willing with God, praying with God, praising with God. Surely it is too much, this last promise. How can God trust us with a power so deep and terrible ? Ah, He can trust the ideal life with anything. " If he ask anything." Well, if he do, he will ask nothing amiss. It will be God's will if it is asked. It will be God's will if it is not asked. For he is come, this man, " *to do God's will*."

(8) There is only one thing more which the model man may ever wish to have. We can imagine him wondering, as he thinks of the unspeakable beauty of this life—of its angelic purity, of its divine glory, of its Christ-like unselfishness, of its heavenly peace—how long this life can last. It may seem too bright and beautiful, for all things fair have soon

to come to an end. And if any cloud could cross the true Christian's sky, it would be when he thought that this ideal life might cease. But God, in the riches of His forethought, has rounded off this corner of his life with a great far-reaching text, which looks above the circumstance of time, and projects his life into the vast eternity beyond. *" He that doeth the will of God abideth for ever "* (1 John ii. 17).

May God grant that you and I may learn to live this great and holy life, remembering the solemn words of Him who lived it first, who only lived it all : " Not every one that saith unto me, Lord, Lord, shall enter into the Kingdom of Heaven ; but he that doeth the will of My Father which is in Heaven."

II.

GOD'S WILL—THE CHRISTIAN'S AIM

GOD'S WILL—THE CHRISTIAN'S AIM

" I came down from Heaven not to do mine
own Will, but the Will of Him that sent me "
(John vi. 38).

THERE are a great many threads on which the
circumstances of human life are strung ; and the
real value of any man's life depends on the thread
and not on the circumstances. All the circumstances
of such a life as Napoleon's, for instance, seem hung
on this thread—Ambition. It was the passion for
power and success that gave it unity. It connected
each apparently stray and scattered event of his
life into a great wedge-like mass which moved
across Europe upturning armies and empires and
thrones. It was another form of ambition, a holy
ambition, running through every detail and circumstance that gave point to Luther's life, or
Knox's, or Cromwell's. The man with a purpose
is the most formidable of men, the statesman with
a policy the most invincible of politicians, and if
there was anything more than another which made
Paul a terror to the heathen world of his time and

a crown of glory to the Christianity of to-day, it lies in this little sentence which he wrote, "This one thing I do."

Every man who ever thought deeply about religion has tried to find out the purpose of the Life of Christ. Many indeed never dream of any underlying principle, and mean no more by the life of Christ than the train of miracle and parable and incident which formed the outward circumstances of his career. But there was a thread to his life. These are just the beads ; and no one can even appreciate circumstance until he first have apprehended principle.

Now there have been hundreds of guesses at the mysterious thread which bound His life together. Like an exquisite piece of tapestry His life showed matchless pictures and incomparable histories ; and men felt strongly curious to find the warp on which these scenes were woven. Nothing so marvellous, so perfect, so unique had ever appeared on the world's stage before. So all the poor players who have come and gone since then that ever heard of this wonderful career have found themselves guessing at the secret of His Life, and asking what He did here.

"He came to teach us the meaning of Self-Denial," says one, "that is the great principle that underlay

His Life. "No," say others, "that is only half a truth; He also came to teach us how to live." "Nay, not to live," say others still; "He came to teach us how to die." But others say, "Not even to teach us how to die. He came to die for us." So men have found far different secrets in His Life. They have searched their minds and libraries; they have constructed theories with profound ability, demolishing others to make room for them with marvellous ingenuity. They have elaborated treatises to prove that He meant this or that He meant that; but if they had gone to Jesus himself to ask Him what it meant, they would have got his answer in these few plain words, "I came down from Heaven to do the Will of Him that sent Me."

You may remember, on last Sabbath, how we found that the same truth ran through the conception of the ideal human life; how the ideal life when dissected, when analysed, when reconstructed on Bible principles, gave this result at every point of investigation, that its aim and scope were always centred somewhere within the Will of God. To-day we leave the analysis of the ideal life in the written word to consider the realisation in the living Word—in the living Person of Christ— to find how He carried out these principles in the every-day things of His Life, so that we who know already to find in Him the ideal for our character may learn what sometimes seems a harder lesson, to find in Him the principle for our conduct. We seek then to-day in the life of the great Ideal, for illustration of the principle that the end of His Life and our life is to do the Will of God.

When we come to apply this to His Life, to see, as it were, if we have found the true key to it, it is very remarkable that this very principle crops up in the first glimpse of His Life we get. For thirty long years of Christ's Life we only know one thing about Him. Only once the curtain is drawn back, and that but for a moment ; yet in that moment a keen observer has time to make this great discovery, that the leading principle of that young life was *to do God's Will.*

He was only twelve years old then, the time when the Jewish youth began to take public part in the religion of their fathers. Joseph and Mary had been wont each year to leave their quiet home in Nazareth, and go up to the great temple of Jerusalem for the Feast of the Passover. This time they take their boy with them. In the bustle of the festal days they miss one another, and the parents journey home without the Son. Hastily they retrace their steps to the Holy City, and after three anxious days they find him in the temple " sitting among the doctors, both hearing them and asking questions." "Behold thy father and I have sought thee sorrowing," the gentle mother says. " Why hast thou dealt thus with us ? " And then the Son gives His deep mysterious answer, " Wist ye not that I must be about my Father's business ?" No, they wist not. In one sense it was the simplest doctrine in the world. God's Will was to be done before His parents'. Yet they could not understand it. They wist it not. We may think it is a hackneyed truth this, that we are here to do God's Will, that we are here to look after our Father's business. We may think that all men know this commonplace as we are inclined to call it ; but it is just the great commonplaces that are universally unknown. Man wist these things not. Small conceits, petty side-lights of truth, so and so's views, and so and so's heresies,—these are the things men really are fond of. But the deep penetrating truths which most people dismiss with an " of course ! " are just the truths the world is last to follow or believe.

Even the worthy Joseph and the good Mary did not know this truth. However far their theology went, it went not so far as this. " They understood not " we are told, " the saying which

he spake unto them." No, they did not understand
Him. No doubt they thought it a mere youthful
imprudence. The boy was precocious, the good
people would say ; the high priests and the doctors
would forgive it ; and they as parents would see
to it that it did not happen again. So has it always
been when any man has dared to do God's Will.
It is always an uncommon thing. People think it
is a commonplace ; the doctrine is, *very*. But the
man who interprets it into action will find himself
doing strange things, and running against the grain
of the world, and deciding things quite differently
from his other wise friends, and being misunderstood perpetually by those who know and love him
best. And of all trials which the true Christian
has to bear this is surely the keenest and sorest,
to be misunderstood in following a lead you dare
not lose which no one follows but yourself.

> " God sometimes will give me a light
>   No other man can see,
>   A light that teaches me a way
>   That's only shewn to me.
>   Then shall I follow on although
>   All else in darkness be,
>   I'd rather let God's Will be done
>   Than men speak well of me."

There was not a man in all that temple probably who could sympathise with what Jesus had done. What could he mean, this lad of twelve, running away from his parents in this manner ? No doubt Nazareth was a dull place for a lad of his years, no doubt there was a great deal of tempting sight-seeing at Jerusalem, but that was no excuse for his leaving his parents. No, no ! And so he is led back in disgrace probably. No one, not even his own parents, understood him, because he did the Will of God.

Such is the Cross the Christian bears who does the Will of God. Oh, it is the most bitter time of a young man's life when in following what he is sure is his Heavenly Father's Will, he has to cross the will of his earthly parents whom in everything else but this he would lay down his life to serve. It is a dreadful thing to have the fifth command-ment quoted for his humiliation when he knows that he is not honouring his father or mother only when that might be dishonouring to God. And what can he say to them but the old pathetic words, " I know that ye wist not, yet I must be about My Father's business."

It is thus a striking and remarkable fact that the first conscious thing we know that Jesus did was to take this stand for the deep principle which

no man sympathised with, that the end of His
life was to do God's will—a truth which was more
to Him than His own prosperity, His father's
counsel, or even the love of His mother. And the
man who follows his Saviour cannot remember with
too much gratitude that the first words of His the
world will ever know, the only words indeed for
thirty long years of His life, were in illustration of
this great principle that in God's Will lies the end
and aim of every human life.

There are several other cases during the short
years of the subsequent ministry, when Jesus
expressly states this principle in words. But
as we are looking at the question from its practical
side, we prefer to read another illustration from His
life than from His lips. And we shall take a case
in which no hint at first of the underlying principle
seems at all to be conveyed, in which the surface
of everyday life seems altogether unbroken by
anything more than the ordinary circumstances
and accidents of the day.

Near the eastern base of the Mount of Olives in
the heart of a quiet, sweet valley lay the little
village of Bethany. In one of its small houses
there lived in these days, we are told, a little family
—two sisters and a brother. It was a hospitable
home, we know, and sometimes when Jesus would

be passing on His way to the Holy City He would find a kindly shelter beneath its roof. So this brother with his sisters got to know Jesus. By and by as the visits became more frequent perhaps, they were numbered with His dearest earthly friends. " And Jesus loved Mary and her sister and Lazarus their brother." One day a dark shadow falls over this little household; the brother is stricken with disease. To whom can the sisters turn in this their hour of need ? Their best friend, Jesus, is far away on the other side of the Jordan. If He only knew how ill their brother was ! He would not mind the journey, He would soon be standing by the bedside of his friend, and as Lazarus does not improve they determine to send for Him. Messengers are sent off in haste, and the hours drag wearily in the sickroom while Martha and Mary watch for their return. Of course He will be with them, they think, and Lazarus will be well. By and by the messengers come back, the sisters run out to meet them, but alas they are alone ! Jesus has not come. What a disappointment ! Why was He not with them ? Was He ill ? Was He a prisoner anywhere ? Had the Jews seized hold of Him at last ? Was He worn out with His labours, and stricken like His friend that He could not come ? No, He was well and safe. They did not know what it meant. He could have come quite well for all that they knew. He had muttered some mysterious words which they could not understand, and gone on with His work again. Oh! what could it mean, this unusual treatment? It was not like Jesus. And when Lazarus hears of it, it makes him worse. He will come yet, the sisters think, but no! Lazarus is dying now. It will be too late even if He come. Still the weeping sisters wait and watch, and watch and wait in the stillness of the chamber till Lazarus is dead. Hours pass, days pass, and still He has not come. Friends have come from all the country round, and mourners from Jerusalem to join them in their grief; but He comes not. He, the best Friend of them all, comes not. Alas! Alas! He does not even send a message to them, not one word of excuse. He was with them in prosperity and now when adversity is come He neglects them, and friends who scarce know them, who never got more than a passing kindness from them, are vieing with one another in words of sympathy and love!

Now where was Jesus all this time? What explanation could He give of His unusual conduct? This inhuman conduct, some of the people would have called it. What excuse could He give for himself? Excuse! He who does God's Will need

never give excuse. That is excuse enough. And
the principle on which Jesus stayed in Peræa when
every one thought it the right thing that He
should be in Bethany was simply this—that the
end of life is not to look after one's sick friends but
to do the Will of God. This is putting the principle
broadly and coarsely, but it brings out what is
meant.

Christ was doing God's Will when the message
reached Him. He might have been resting or
working or teaching or preaching. He might have
been doing something which seemed very important
or very unimportant. But no matter what it
seemed, it was God's Will He was doing, therefore
it was important. Your life and mine may seem
unimportant to the world. But it matters little
how it seems. It is *tremendously* important if we
are doing God's Will, be it only a round of paltry
duties and everyday routine.

When Jesus heard that Lazarus was sick, no
doubt the readiest impulse of His heart was to go
to Bethany at once. But this was not the highest
impulse—only the readiest. In Him and in every
true follower He has, above all personal ends,
above even the divine and beautiful desires of
natural affection, there is the overmastering
impulse to do the Will of God. That may lie along

the line of natural affection, or it may not. The impulse of love, or the incident that evokes it, may be the indication of God's Will, or it may not. That is exactly what the Christian has to find out, and what he can only find out, and cannot fail to find out, if he is willing to accept any alternative which God may choose to offer him, if he recognises, as Christ did, that he was here for this one cause, to do the Will of Him who sent him.

Of course this does not mean that ordinary duties are to be neglected and family affection crushed. It may be God's Will in ninety-nine cases out of every hundred that a summons coming in such circumstances should be immediately complied with, and probably it would be so. Still this is not the question; it is not the general question of family affection being instituted by God and respected by God, and therefore to be indicative of what His Will may be. That may be quite true, but it is the particular question, not that family and friendly ties are to be held as ends in life, but solely and entirely the doing of God's Will,—the doing of God's Will whether that run alongside family affection or cut across it, the doing of God's Will in public things or private things, in social things, or personal, in great things or little things, especially in very little things where the temptation is to neglect them as insignificant, or in very great things where the tendency to make the urgency of the emergency a substitute for God's Will is one of the subtlest and most dangerous of snares. Emergencies may be indicative of God's Will or they may not. But it is not the strength of the emergency that is to guide us, but the direction of God's Will at that particular time.

It was very hard one might say that Christ was denied the privilege of ministering to His friend —that His friend in that dark hour should miss the grasp of that Hand or the soothing tones of His voice. It was hard that confiding Mary should be forgotten, and busy Martha be unrewarded for all the service she had done Him. But these were not the things for which Christ came here. " I came down from Heaven not to do what I liked, or what Lazarus liked, or Mary liked or Martha liked, but to do the Will of Him that sent Me."

Contrast with this for a moment how any of us would have been likely to have acted, how all our good friends would have recommended us to have acted. Suppose on going home from Church to-day you found a telegram telling you that your dearest earthly friend had been seized with sudden and dangerous illness. The immediate impulse would be to fly to that bedside without a moment's loss of time. But this might be simply doing either your own will, or the sick friend's will, or the friends of the sick friend's will. It might be God's Will or it might not. *That* is the first thing to be found out; not what you wish, or they wish. God may have something for you to do here to-day, perhaps only three little boys to teach in a class—perhaps only to set a good example to some one for an hour or two, perhaps to teach you patience, or even how to pray for the absent friend. Perhaps if you went it would be to take infection yourself; perhaps the train by which you went might come into collision, or a thousand other things which you could not foresee. If God wants these things to come upon you, let it be so. If He wants you to go and nothing come upon you, or to stay and do some good or no good, let it be so. Only let God's hand be in it. That is the whole lesson of it. Whatever your decision may be, let it be based on what is God's Will. In all thy ways acknowledge God, and He shall direct thy path. Whatsoever ye do, do all in the name of the Lord. For the end of life, once more, is not for us to love or refrain from loving, to work or wait, to rejoice or suffer, to live or die, but to do God's Will.

Perhaps you are asking, but what are we to make of circumstances? Are we not to be guided by circumstances ? Well, we are just to make of circumstances what God makes of them. Sometimes He will reveal His will through circumstances and sometimes He will not. Sometimes circumstances may be a mere temptation to us. Sometimes they may be sent us simply to see whether we are following circumstances or following the Will of God. If Christ had followed circumstances, probably He would have rushed off to Bethany as soon as He heard the news that Lazarus was ill. But how then are we to know the Will of God, how are we to detect it in circumstance, or know when it is absent—these are great and important questions, but they are not before us now. It is sufficient for us to know that God has given His promise of absolute and unerring direction to every sincere and honest heart which really seeks His will.

Of course if we act on these principles most people will misunderstand us. We must be prepared for this. They will say it is preposterous being so very particular about everything we do. That what we do is of no greater importance than what anyone else does, that we are just making life a bondage and that we should just comport ourselves as nearly as possible like other and better people. Taunts of this kind are exceedingly hard to bear— all the more so that they generally come from those who are supposed to be likewise the followers of Christ. An abuse of this principle may indeed be a bondage, may lead to the grossest lawlessness and sin. But the principle itself can never be a bondage. It is the most complete freedom. If it is applied intermittently it may be a bondage —when special occasions arise, for instance. But a spasmodic principle is no principle. It is a religious caprice. To be truly valuable it must run through the whole life, be the thread on which everything else is strung, till it becomes the truest purpose of the heart that the Will of God be done. Christ, no doubt, was very much misunderstood even in this very instance. The messengers would misunderstand him, and Martha and Mary, and probably the disciples who were with Him, must have wondered what He meant. But He was accustomed to this. 'Tis because He was accustomed to walk by a light that others could seldom see. All His life He had been misunderstood,—by His disciples, by His relations, by His enemies, by His friends. Yes, and He could even remember a bitterer time than all, when his own Mother said He was mad.

Finally, there is a glorious sequel to this tale. God's Will is always best. He knows the end from the beginning. Just see what Jesus got by waiting.

Had He rushed off at once, Lazarus would still have been in life. A touch from His finger would have cured him. It would have been a great miracle. It would have brought great glory to God Yet by waiting, Christ wrought more than a great miracle —He wrought the greatest of miracles. It was the climax of miracles. He would have brought glory to God had He gone at first : by waiting He brought great glory to God It was one of the most glorious triumphs of His life.

After getting the message, Jesus just went on with His work. A day passed, another day, two whole days, and yet He had not started. He was waiting God's time. God always provides the opportunity as well as the call to work. At length He starts. He is in no hurry. He is doing God's will. If it was God's Will that He should go faster, He would do it. God may have had many things for Him to do on the road. At all events when He arrived at the sad little home in Bethany, His friend had been long dead and buried. Four whole days he had been in his grave. Now see what this meant. The miracle of the raising of Lazarus has ever been the greatest stumbling block to sceptics. For many centuries a perfect storm of unbelief has raged around it. It is one of the foci of rationalism. Renan in France, Strauss, Schleiermacher and

Schentsel in Germany, have vied with one another in constructing ingenious theories to prove it was a trance, a swoon, a peculiar species of fit. But Christ's waiting there four days for ever dismisses such blinded views as these. When He arrived, the Bible says, " he stinketh." The finger of decay is quick in Eastern lands. Corruption had set in. No doubt that he was dead. So, waiting on God's Will, Christ wrought the crowning wonder of His life.

Thus we have caught a glimpse of the ruling passion of the ideal human life. May God cut channels deep in your life and in mine, in which the Will of God may flow for evermore ! May He keep us from doing what our poor thoughts imagine to be best, and give us a deeper principle on which to construct to-morrow's wishes and the next day's plans than what will please ourselves ! And may we remember the example of Him of whom it is written " He pleased not Himself " ; who said, as He drained the bitterest cup that ever was filled with sorrow or with sin, " Nevertheless not My Will, but thine O Lord be done."

One word more. These are the truths which God generally teaches us through trouble. He has to do it. We will not learn them when life is soft and rich. And He has to take it away and make it poor and hard. The widows learn these things in the sad moment of mourning ; the fatherless read them as they stand by the open graves. But let those of us who are strong and well and satisfied with life take solemn heed this day to do this Will of God, lest He have to teach us through sorrow and tribulation and tears.

III.

WHAT IS GOD'S WILL?

WHAT IS GOD'S WILL?

" The God of our fathers hath chosen thee, that
thou shouldest know His will."—ACTS xxii. 14.

WE resume to-day a subject, the thread of which
has been broken by the interval of a few Sabbaths—
the subject of the Will of God.

Already we have tried to learn two lessons :—

1. That the end of our life is to do the will of God.

2. That this was the end of Christ's life.

It will help to recall what has gone before if we
compare this with another definition of the end
of life with which we are all familiar.

Of course this is not the most complete statement
of the end of our life ; but it is the most practical,
and it will recall the previous conclusions if we
refer to this for a moment.

Our Shorter Catechism, for instance, puts the
end of life quite in different words. " Man's chief
end," it says, " is to glorify God and enjoy Him
for ever." But this answer is just too great for us.
There is too much in it. It is really the same
answer, but turned towards God. It is too great

245

to understand. It is as true, but too profoundly true. It is wonderfully conceived and put together, but it goes past us. It expresses the end of life God-ward—determines the quality of all the things we do by the extent to which they make way in the world for the everywhere coming glory of God. But this is too wonderful for us. We want a principle *life-ward* as well as God-ward. We want something to tell us what to do with the things beneath us and around us and within us, as well as the things above us. Therefore there is a human side to the Shorter Catechism's answer.

What is the chief end of man ?

Man's chief end is to do the will of God.

In one sense this is not such a divine answer. But we are not divine. We understand God's will : God's glory, only faintly—we are only human yet, and " glory " is a word for heaven.

Ask a schoolboy, learning the first question in the Catechism, to do a certain thing for the glory of God. The opportunity of doing the thing may be gone before the idea can be driven into the boy's head of what the glory of God means. But tell him to do the thing because it is God's will that he should do it—he understands that. He knows that God's will is just what God likes, and what he himself probably does *not* like. And the

conception of it from this side is so clear that no
schoolboy even need miss the end of life—for that
is simply doing what God likes. If our souls are
not great enough, then, to think of God's glory as
the practical rule of life, let them not be too small
to think of God's will.   And if we look after the
end of life from this side, God will from the other.
Do we the will of God, God will see that it glorifies
God.

Let us suppose, then, that after casting about
for an object in life, we have at last stopped at
this—the end of my life is to do the will of God.
Let us suppose also that we have got over the disappointment of finding that there is nothing
higher for us to do in the world. Or, perhaps,
taking the other side, suppose we are beginning
to feel the splendid conviction that, after all, our
obscure life is not to be wasted : that having this
ideal principle within it, it may yet be as great
in its homely surroundings as the greatest human
life,—seeing that no man can do more with his
life than the will of God,—that though we may
never be famous or powerful, or called to heroic
suffering or acts of self-denial which will vibrate
through history : that though we are neither
intended to be apostles nor missionaries nor martyrs
—but to be common people living ·in common

houses, spending the day in common offices or
common kitchens, yet doing the will of God
there, we shall do as much as apostle or
missionary or martyr—seeing that they can do
no more than do God's will where they are, even
as we can do as much where we are—and answer
the end of our life as truly, faithfully, and
triumphantly as they.

Suppose we feel all this, and desire, as we stand
on the threshold of the truly ideal life, that, God
helping us, we shall live it if we may, we are met
at once with the question, How are we ever to
know what the will of God can be ? The chief
end of life is to do the will of God *Question :* How
am I to know the will of God—to know it clearly
and definitely ? Is it possible ? and if so,
how ?

Now, to begin with, we have probably an opinion
on the matter already. And if you were to express it,
it would be this : that it is not possible. You have
thought about the will of God, and read and thought
and thought and read, and you have come to
this conclusion, that the will of God is a very
mysterious thing—a very mysterious thing,
which some people may have revealed to
them, but does not seem in any way possible to
you.

Your nature is different from other people's; and though you have strained your eyes in prayer and thought, you have never seen the will of God yet. And if you ever have been in the same line with it, it has only been by chance, for you can see no principle in it, nor any certainty of ever being in the same line again. One or two special occasions, indeed, you can recall when you thought you were near the will of God, but they must have been special interpositions on God's part. He does not show His will every day like that : once or twice only in a life-time, that is as much of this high experience as one ever dare expect.

Now, of course, it is no use going on to find out what God's will is if the thing is impossible. If this experience is correct—and we cannot know God's will for the mystery of it—we may as well give up the ideal life at once. But if you examined this experience, even cursorily, you would find at once how far away from the point it is.

1. In the first place, it is merely an experience ; it is exclusively based on your own experience, not on God's thoughts regarding it, but on your own thoughts. The true name for this is presumption.

2. It assumes that, the end of life being to do God's will, and you not being able to know God's

will, are therefore not responsible for fulfilling the end of life. This is self-deception.

3. It suggests the idea that God could teach you His will if He liked, seeing that He had done so once or twice by your own admission. And yet, though He wishes you to do His will, and you wish it too, He deliberately refuses to tell you what it is. This is an accusation against God.

It is something worse than unreasonable, therefore, to say that we think it hopeless for us ever to know God's will. On the contrary, indeed, there is a strong presumption that we should find it out. For if it is so important a thing that the very end of life is involved in it, it would be absurd to imagine that God should ever keep us the least in the dark as to what His will may mean.

And this presumption is changed into a certainty when we balance our minds for a moment on the terms of this text, "The God of our fathers hath chosen thee, that thou shouldest know His will." It is not simply a matter of presumption, it is a matter of election. Have you ever thought of this strange, deep calling of God ? We are called to salvation, we have thought of that ; we are called to holiness, we have thought of that ; but as great as either is this, we are called to know

God's will. We are answering our call in other ways ; are we answering it in this ? What is God's will ? Are we knowing God's will ? How much have we learned of that to which we have been called ? And is it our prayer continually, as it was his to whom these words were said, that we may be " filled with the knowledge of His will " ?

It is a reasonable object of search, then, to find out what God's will for us may be. And it is a reasonable expectation that we may find it out so fully as to know at any moment whether we be in the line of it or no ; and when difficulty arises about the next step of our life, we may have absolute certainty which way God's will inclines. There are many kinds of assurance in religion ; and it is as important to have assurance of God's will as to have assurance of God's salvation. For just as the loss of assurance of salvation means absence of peace and faith, and usefulness, so absence of assurance of God's will means miserable Christian life, imperfect Christian character, and impaired Christian usefulness.

We start our investigation, therefore, in the belief that God *must* have light for all of us on the subject of His will, and with the desire to have assurance in the guidance of our life by God as clear and strong as of its redemption and salvation by Christ.

In one sense, of course, no man can know the will of God, even as in one sense no man can know God Himself. God's will is a great and infinite mystery—a thing of mighty mass and volume, which can no more be measured out to hungry souls in human sentences than the eternal knowledge of God or the boundless love of Christ. But even as there is a sense in which one poor human soul can hold enough of the eternal knowledge of God and the boundless love of Christ, so is there a sense in which God can put as much of His will into human words as human hearts can bear—as much as human wills can will or human lives perform.

When we come to put this will into words, we find that it divides itself into two great parts.

I. There is a part of God's will which every one may know—*a universal part*.

II. A part of God's will which no one knows but you—*a particular part*.

A universal part—for every one. A particular part—for the individual.

I. To begin with the first. There is a part of God's will which every one may know. It is written in Divine characters in two sacred books, which

every man may read. The one of them is the Bible,
the other is Nature. The Bible is God's will in words,
in formal thoughts, in grace. Nature is God's will
in matter and tissue and force. Nature is not often
considered a part of God's will. But it is a part,
and a great part, and the first part. And perhaps
one reason why some never know the second is
because they yield no full obedience to the first.
God's law of progress is from the lower to the higher;
and scant obedience at the beginning of His will
means disobedience with the rest. The laws of
nature are the will of God for our bodies. As there
is a will of God for our higher nature—the moral
laws—as emphatically is there a will of God for
the lower—the natural laws. If you would know
God's will in the higher, therefore, you must
begin with God's will in the lower : which simply
means this—that if you want to live the ideal
life, you must begin with the ideal body. The law
of moderation, the law of sleep, the law of regularity,
the law of exercise, the law of cleanliness—this is the
law or will of God for you. This is the first law, the
beginning of His will for you. And if we are
ambitious to get on to do God's will in the higher
reaches, let us respect it as much in the lower ;
for there may be as much of God's will in minor
things, as much of God's will in taking good bread

and pure water, as in keeping a good conscience
or living a pure life. Whoever heard of gluttony
doing God's will, or laziness, or uncleanness, or
the man who was careless and wanton of natural
life ? Let a man disobey God in these, and you
have no certainty that he has any true principle
for obeying God in anything else : for God's will
does not only turn into the church and the prayer-
meeting and the higher chambers of the soul, but
into the common rooms at home down to wardrobe
and larder and cellar, and into the bodily frame
down to blood and muscle and brain

This, then, is the first contribution to the contents of the will of God. And, for distinction,
they may be called the *physical contents*

Next in order we come to the *moral contents*,
both of these coming under the same head as parts
of God's will which every one may know.

These moral contents, as we have seen, are
contained in the Word of God ; and the Bible has a
variety of names for them, such as testimonies,
laws, precepts, statutes, commandments.

Now this is a much more formidable array than
the physical contents. It is one thing to be in
physical condition—a prize-fighter may be that
—but it is quite another to be in moral condition.
And it is a difficult matter to explain exactly what

God's will in this great sense is ; for, on the one hand, there is the danger of elevating it so high as to frighten the timid soul from ever attempting to reach it, and, on the other, the insensible tendency to lower it to human standards and aims.

It must be understood, however, to the full that, as far as its formidableness is concerned, that is absolutely unchangeable. God's moral law cannot be toned down into anything less binding, less absolutely moral, less infinitely significant. Whatever it means, is meant for every man in its rigid truth as the definite and formal expression of God's will for him.

From the moral side there are three different departments of God's will. Foremost, and apparently most rigid of all, are the Ten Commandments. Now the Ten Commandments contain, in a few sentences, one of the largest-known portions of God's will. They form the most strict code of morality in the world : the basis of all others, the most venerable and universal expression of the will of God for man. Following upon this there come the Beatitudes of Christ. This is another large portion of God's will. This forms the most unique code of morality in the world, the most complete and lovely additional expression of the will of God for Christians. Passing through the human heart of Christ, the older commandment of the Creator becomes the soft and mellow beatitude of the Saviour—passes from the colder domain of law with a penalty on failure, to the warm region of love with a benediction on success. These are the two chief elements in the moral part of the will of God for man. But there is a third set of laws and rules, which are not to be found exactly expressed in either of these. The Ten Commandments and the Beatitudes take up most of the room in God's will, but there are shades of precept still unexpressed which also have their place. Hence we must add to all this mass of law and beatitude many more laws and many more beatitudes which lie enclosed in other texts, and other words of Christ, which have their place like the rest as portions of God's will.

Here, then, we already know a great part of what God's will is ; although, perhaps, we have not often called it by this name. And it may be worth while, before going on to find out any more, to pause for a moment and find out how to practise this.

For, perhaps, when we see how great a thing it is, this will of God, our impulse for the moment is

to wish we had not known. We were building ourselves up with the idea that we were going to try
this life, and that it was easy and smooth compared
with the life we left. There was a better future
opening to us, with visions of happiness and
holiness and even of usefulness to God. But our
hopes are dashed now. How can we do God's will ?
—this complicated mass of rules and statutes, each
bristling with the certainty of a thousand breakages?
How can we keep these ten grave laws, with their
unflinching scorn of compromise and exacting
obligation, to the uttermost jot and tittle ? How
can our coarse spirits breathe the exquisite air of
these beatitudes, or fit our wayward wills to the
narrow mould of all these binding texts ? Can God
know how weak we are, and blind and biassed
towards the breakages, ere ever we thought of
Him ? Can He think how impossible it is to keep
these laws, even for one close-watched, experi-
mental hour ? Did Christ really mean it—not some
lesser thing than this—when He taught in the ideal
prayer that God's will was to be done on earth *even
as* it is done in heaven ?

There can be but one answer. " God hath chosen
thee, that thou shouldest know His will." And God
expects from each of us neither less nor more than
this. He knows the frailty of our frame ; He

remembers we are dust. And yet such dust that He has given each of us the divinest call to the vastest thing in heaven. There, by the side of our frailty, He lays down His holy will—lays it down confidingly, as if a child could take it in its grasp, and, as if He means the child to fondle it and bear it in its breast, He says, " If a man love Me, he will keep My words."

There must be something, therefore, to ease the apparent hopelessness of doing this will of God —something to give us heart to go on with it, to give strength to obey God's call. We were not prepared to find it running in to the roots of things like this ; but there must be something brighter somewhere than the dark side we have seen. Well, then, let us think for a moment on these points.

1. In the first place, there *must* be such laws. God is a King—His kingdom the kingdom of heaven. His people are His subjects. Subjects must have laws. Therefore we start with a necessity. Laws must be.

2. But who are afraid of laws ? Good subjects ? Never. Criminals are afraid of laws. Who dread the laws of this country, cry out against them, and would abolish them if they could ? Drunkards, thieves, murderers. Who love the laws of this

country ? The honest, the wise and good. Then who are afraid of God's laws—would abolish them if they could ? The wicked, the profligate, the licentious. But *you* would not. The just and holy, the pure in heart and life love them, respect them. More still, they demand them. It would be no kingdom without them—no kingdom worth belonging to. If it were not for its laws of truth and purity, and its promise of protection from unrighteousness and sin, it would have no charm for them. It is the inaccessible might and purity of will in the kingdom of God that draw all other wills as subjects to its sway. It is not only not hard, therefore, that there should be such elements in God's will as law ; it is a privilege. And it is more than a privilege to have them.

3. It is a privilege to do them. And it is a peculiar privilege, this. It consists partly in forgetting that they are laws—in changing their names, commandment, precept, testimony, statute, into this—the will of God. No sternness then can enter with the thought, for God's name is in the name, and the help of God, and the power of God, and the constraining love of Christ. This takes away the hopelessness of trying to keep God's will. It makes it a personal thing, a relation to a living will, not to didactic law.

And there is, further, a wonderful provision near it. When God puts down His great will beside me telling me to do it, He puts down just beside it as great a thing, His Love. And as my soul trembles at the fearfulness of will, Love comes with its calm omnipotence, and draws it to Himself ; then takes my timid will and twines it around His, till mine is fierce with passion to serve, and strong to do His will. Just as if some mighty task were laid to an infant's hand, and the engine-grasp of a giant strengthened it with his own. Where God's law is, is God's love. Look at Law—it withers your very soul with its stern, inexorable face. But look at Love, or look at God's will, which means look at Love's will, and you are re-assured, and your heart grows strong. No martyr dies for abstract truth. For a person, for God, he will die a triple death. So no man will die for God's law. But for God he will do it. Where God's will, then, seems strong to command, God's love is strong to obey. Hence the profound texts, " Love is the fulfilling of the law." " And this is the love of God that we keep His commandments, and His commandments are not grievous."

God's will, then, is as great as God, as high as heaven, yet as easy as love. For love knows no hardness, and feels no yoke. It desires no yielding to its poverty in anything it loves. Let God be greater, and His will sterner, love will be stronger and obedience but more true. Let not God come down to me: slacken truth for me, make His will weaker for me: my interests, as subject, are safer with my King, are greater with the greatness of my King—only give me love, pure, burning love of and loyalty to Him, and I shall climb from law to law through grace and glory, to the place beside the throne where the angels do His will. There are two ways, therefore, of looking at God's will —one looking at the love side of it, the other at the law ; the one ending in triumph, the other in despair ; the one a liberty, the other a slavery. And you might illustrate this in a simple way, to make it finally clear,—for this is the hardest point to hold,—in some such way as this.

Suppose you go into a workshop occasionally, and watch the workmen at their task. The majority do their work in an uninterested, mechanical sort of way. Everything is done with the most proper exactness and precision—almost with slavish precision, a narrower watch would say. They come exactly at the hour in the morning, and throw down their work to a second exactly when the closing bell has rung. There is a certain punctiliousness about them, and a scrupulosity about their work ; and as part cause of it, perhaps, you observe an uncomfortable turning of the head occasionally as if some eye were upon them, then a dogged going on of their work again, as if it were always done under some restraint.

But among the workmen you will notice one who seems to work on different principles. There is a buoyancy and cheerfulness about him as he goes about his work, which is foreign to all the rest. You will see him at his place sometimes even before the bell has rung, and if unfinished work be in his hands when closing time has come, he does not mind an extra five minutes when all the others are gone. What strikes you about him is the absence of that punctiliousness which marked the others' work. It does not seem at all a tyranny to him, but even a freedom and a pleasure ; and though he is apparently not so mechanical in his movements as his mates, his work seems better done and greater, despite the ease and light-heartedness which mark him through its course. Now the difference between them is this. The first set of men are hired workmen. The man by himself is the master's son. Not that he is outwardly different ; he is a common workman in a fustian jacket like the rest. But he is the master's son. The first set work for wages, come in at regulation hours lest aught be kept off their wages, keep the workshop laws in terror of losing their place. But the son keeps them, and keeps them better, not for wages, but for love.

So the Christian keeps the will or the laws of God because of the love of God. Not because they are workshop regulations framed and hung up before him at every moment of his life but because they are his Master's will. They are as natural to him as air. He would never think of not keeping them. His meat is to do the will of his Father which is in heaven. There is no room for punctiliousness in this the true way of doing God's will. A scrupulous Christian is a hired servant, and not the Master's son.

II. But now, very briefly, in the second and last place, there is an unknown part of God's will— at least, a part which is only known to *you*. There is God's will for the world, and God's will for the individual. There is God's will written on tables of stone for all the world to read. There is God's will carved in sacred hieroglyphic which no one reads but you. There is God's will rolling in thunder over the life of universal man. There is God's will dropped softly on the believer's ear in angel whispers or spoken by the still small voice within. This, the final element in God's will, to distinguish

it from the moral and physical contents which go
before, one might call the more strictly *spiritual*
content.

This is a distinct addition to the other parts—
an addition, too, which many men ignore, and
other men deny. But there is such a region in
God's will—a region unmapped in human charts,
unknown to human books, a region for the pure in
heart, for the upright, for the true. It is a land of
mystery to those who know it not, a land of foolish-
ness, and weaknesses, and delusive sights and
sounds. But there is a land where the Spirit
moves, a luminous land, a walking in God's light.
There is a region where God's own people have
their breathing from above, where each saint's
steps are ordered of the Lord.

Now this region may be distinguished from the
other regions by its secrecy. It is a private thing ;
between God and you. You want to know what to
do next—your calling in life, for instance. You
want to know what action to take in a certain
matter. You want to know what to do with your
money. You want to know whether to go into a
certain scheme or not. Then you enter into this
private chamber of God's will, and ask the private
question, " Lord, what wouldest Thou have *me*
to do ? "

Then it is distinguished by its action. It concerns a different department of our life. The first part of God's will, all that has gone before, affects our *character*. But this affects something more. It affects our *career*. And this is an important distinction. A man's career in life is almost as important as his character in life ; that is to say, it is almost as important to God, which is the real question. If character is the end of life, then the ideal career is just where character can best be established and developed. A man is to live for his character. But if God's will is the end of life, God may have a will for my career as well as for my character, which does not mean that a man is to live for his career, but for God's will *in* his character *through* his career.

I may want to put all my work upon my character. But God may want my work for something else. He may want to use me, for instance ; I may not know why, or when, or how, or for whom. But it is possible He may need me, for something or other at some time or other. It may be all through my life, or at some particular part of my life which may be past now, or may be still to come. At all events, I must hold myself in readiness and let Him trace my path ; for though it does not look now as if He had anything for me to do, the next turn of the road may bring it ; so I must watch the turnings of the road for God. Even for the chance of God needing me it is worth while doing this—the chance of Him needing me even once. There is a man in Scripture whom God perhaps used but once. He may have done many other things for God ; still, there was one thing God gave him to do so far overshadowing all other things that he seems to have done but this. He seems, indeed, to have been born, to have lived and died for this. It is the only one thing we know about him. But it is a great thing. His name was Ananias. He was the instrument in the conversion of Paul. What was he doing in Damascus that day, when Paul arrived under conviction of sin ? Why was he living in Damascus at all ? Because he was born there, and his father before him, perhaps you will say. Let it be so. A few will be glad to cherish a higher thought. He was a good man, and his steps were ordered—by ordinary means, if you like—by the Lord. Could Ananias not have been as good a man in Jericho or Antioch, or Ephesus ? Quite as good. His character might almost have been the same. But his career would have been different. And, possibly, his character might have been different from the touch of God upon his career. For when God comes into a man's career, it sometimes makes a mighty difference on his character—teaches him to live less for character and for himself, and more for his career and for God, rather more for both—more for his character by living more for his career. Gold is gold wherever it is ; but it is some difference to the world whether it make a communion cup or gild the proscenium of a theatre.

There is a difference, then, between God in character and God in career. You may have God in your character without having God in your career. Perhaps you should have been in London to-day, perhaps in China. Perhaps you should have been a missionary ; perhaps you should be one yet. Perhaps you should have been in poorer circumstances, or in a different business altogether. Perhaps you have chosen a broader path than God would have willed for yon. Your character may not seem to have suffered ; but your career has. You may be doing God's will with one hand consecrated to Christ, and making your own autobiography with the other consecrated to self.

Would you know the will of God, then ? Consult God about your career. It does not follow because He has done nothing with you last week or last year, He may have nothing for you now. God's

will in career is mostly an unexpected thing—it
comes as a surprise. God's servants work on short
notices. Paul used to have to go off to what was
the end of the world in those days, on a few hours'
warning. And so may you and I. It is not a thing
to startle us, to alarm us, to make us say, " If this
might be the upshot we would let God's will alone."
It would be a wonderful privilege to come to you
or me ; yes, a wonderful privilege that He should
count us worthy to suffer this or anything more
for Him.

But you are old, you say. Ananias was old. Or
steeped in a profession. Paul was steeped in a
profession. Or you are inexperienced and young.
A lad came to Jesus once with five loaves and two
small fishes ; but they fed five thousand men.
So bring your lad's experience, your young offer of
service, and God may use you to twice five thousand
souls. That does not mean that you are to do it.
But be in God's counsels, and He will teach you
whether or no.

How are you to know this secret will of God ?
It is a great question. We cannot touch it now. Let
this suffice. It can be known. It can be known to
you. The steps of a good man are ordered by the
Lord. " I will guide thee with Mine eye." Unto
the upright in heart He shall cause light to arise in

darkness. This is no mysticism, no visionary's
dream. It is not to drown the reason with enthusiasm's airy hope or supersede the word of
God with fanaticism's blind caprice. No, it is not
that. It is what Christ said, " The sheep hear His
voice, and He calleth His own sheep by name,
and leadeth them."

IV.

HOW TO KNOW THE WILL OF GOD

HOW TO KNOW THE WILL OF GOD

" If any man will do His will, he shall know of the
doctrine, whether it be of God."—JOHN vii. 17.

THERE is an experience which becomes more and
more familiar to every one who is trying to follow
Christ—a feeling of the growing loneliness of his
Christian life. It comes from a sense of the
peculiarly personal interest which Christ takes in
him, which sometimes seems so strong as almost to
make him feel that his life is being detached from
all the other lives around him, that it is being drawn
out of the crowd of humanity, as if an unseen arm
linked in his were taking him aside for a nearer
intimacy and a deeper and more private fellowship. It is not, indeed, that the great family of
God are to be left in the shade for him, or that he
is in any way the favourite of heaven ; but it is
the sanctifying and, in the truest sense, humbling
realisation that God makes Himself as real to each
poor unit as if he were the whole ; so that even as
in coming to Christ at first he felt himself the only
lost, so now in staying with Christ he feels himself

the only found. And it is, perhaps, true that without any loss in the feeling of saintly communion with all those throughout the world who say " Our Father " with him in their prayers, the more he feels that Christ has all of him to Himself, the more he feels that he has Christ all to himself. Christ has died for other men, but in a peculiar sense for him. God has a love for all the world, but a peculiar love for him. God has an interest in all the world, but a peculiar interest in him. This is always the instinct of a near fellowship, and it is true of the universal fellowship of God with His own people.

But if there is one thing more than another which is more personal to the Christian—more singularly his than God's love or God's interest—one thing which is a finer symbol of God's love and interest, it is the knowledge of God's will—the private knowledge of God's will. And this is more personal, just inasmuch as it is more private. My private portion of God's love is only a private *share* in God's love—only a part—the same in quality and kind as all the rest of God's love, which all the others get from God. But God's will is a thing for myself. There is a will of God for me which is willed for no one else besides. It is not a share in the universal will, in the same sense as I have a share in the universal love. It is a particular will for me, different from the will He has for anyone else—a private will—a will which no one else knows about, which no one can know about, but me.

To be sure, as we have seen before, God had likewise a universal will for me and every man. In the Ten Commandments, in conscience, in the beatitudes of Christ, God tells all the world His will. There is no secret about this part, it is as universal as His love. It is the will on which the character of every man is to be formed and conformed to God's.

But there is a will for career as well as for character. There is a will for *where*—in what place, viz., in this town or another town—I am to become like God as well as *that* I am to become like God. There is a will for where I am to be, and what I am to be, and what I am to do to-morrow. There is a will for what scheme I am to take up, and what work I am to do for Christ, and what business arrangements to make, and what money to give away. This is God's private will for me, for every step I take, for the path of life along which He points my way : God's will for my *career*.

If I have God's will in my character, my life may become great and good. It may be useful and honourable, and even a monument of the sanctifying power of God. But it will only be a life. However great and pure it be it can be no more than a life. And it ought to be a mission. There should be no such thing as a Christian life, each life should be a mission.

God has a life-plan for every human life. In the eternal counsels of His will, when He arranged the destiny of every star, and every sand-grain and grass-blade, and each of those tiny insects which live but for an hour, the Creator had a thought for you and me. Our life was to be the slow unfolding of this thought, as the corn-stalk from the grain of corn, or the flower from the gradually opening bud. It was a thought of what we were to be, of what we might become, of what He would have us do with our days and years, our influence and our lives. But we all had the terrible power to evade this thought, and shape our lives from another thought, from another will, if we chose. The bud could only become a flower, and the star revolve in the orbit God had fixed. But it was man's prerogative to choose his path, his duty to choose it in God. But the Divine right to choose at all has always seemed more to him than his duty to choose in God, so, for the most part, he has taken his life from God, and cut his career for himself.

It comes to pass, therefore, that there are two great classes of people in the world of Christians to-day. (1) Those who have God's will in their character; (2) Those who have God's will likewise in their career. The first are in the world to live. They have a *life*. The second are in the world to minister. They have a *mission*.

Now those who belong to the first class, those who are simply living in the world and growing character, however finely they may be developing their character, cannot understand too plainly that they are not fulfilling God's will. They are really outside a great part of God's will altogether. They understand the universal part, they are moulded by it, and their lives as lives are in some sense noble and true. But they miss the private part, the secret whispering of God in the ear, the constant message from earth to heaven. " Lord, what wilt Thou have me to do ? " They never have the secret joy of asking a question like this, the wonderful sense in asking it, of being in the counsels of God, the overpowering thought that God has taken notice of you, and your question— that He will let you do something, something peculiar, personal, private, which no one else has been given to do—this thought which gives life for God its true sublimity, and makes a perpetual sacrament of all its common things. Life to them is at the best a bare and selfish thing, for the truest springs of action are never moved at all; and the strangest thing in human history, the bounding of the career from step to step, from circumstance to circumstance, from tragedy to tragedy, is unexplained and unrelated, and hangs, a perpetual mystery, over life.

The great reason possibly why so few have thought of taking God into their career is that so few have really taken God into their life. No one ever thinks of having God in his career, or need think, until his life is fully moulded into God's. And no one will succeed in knowing even what God in his career can mean till he know what it is to have God in the secret chambers of his heart. It requires a well-kept life to know the will of God, and none but the Christlike in character can know the Christlike in career.

It has happened, therefore, that the very fact of God's guidance in the individual life has been denied. It is said to give life an importance quite foreign to the Divine intention in making man. One life, it is argued, is of no more importance than any other life, and to talk of special providences happening every hour of every day is to detract from the majesty and dignity of God; in fact, it reduces a religious life to a mere religious caprice, and the thought that God's will is being done to a hallucination of the mind.

And there is another side to the objection, which though less pronounced and definite, is subtly dangerous still—that there does indeed seem to be some warrant in Scripture for getting to know the will of God ; but that, in the first place, that probably means only on great occasions which come once or twice in a lifetime ; and, in the second, that the whole subject is so obscure that, all things considered, a man had better walk by his own common sense, and leave such mysteries alone.

But the Christian cannot allow the question to be put off with poor evasions like these. Every day, indeed, and many times a day, the question rises in a hundred practical forms. " What is the will of God for me ? " What is the will of God for me to-day, just now, for the next step, for this arrangement and for that, and this amusement, and this projected work for Christ ? For all these he feels he must consult the will of God ; and that God has a will for him in all such things, and that it must be possible somehow to know what that will is, is not only a matter of hope, but a point in his doctrine and creed.

Now without stopping to vindicate the reasonableness of such expectations as these, it may simply be affirmed as a matter of fact that there are a number of instruments for finding out the will of God. One of them is a very great instrument, so far surpassing all the rest in accuracy that there may be said to be but one which has never been known to fail. The others are smaller and clumsier, much less delicate, indeed, and often fail. They often fail to come within sight of the will of God at all, and are so far astray at other times as to mistake some other thing for it. Still they are instruments, and notwithstanding their defects, have a value by themselves, and when the greater instrument employs their humbler powers to second its attempts, they immediately become as keen and as unerring as itself.

The most important of these minor instruments is Reason, and although it is a minor instrument, it is great enough in many a case to reveal the secret will of God. God is taking your life and character through a certain process, for example. He is running your career along a certain chain of events. And sometimes the light which He is showing you stops, and you have to pick your way for a few steps by the dimmer light of thought. But it is God's will for you then to use this thought, and to elevate it through regions of consecration, into faith, and to walk by this light till the clearer beam from His will comes back again.

Another of these instruments is Experience. There are many paths in life which we all tread more than once. God's light was by us when we walked them first, and lit a beacon here and there along the way. But the next time He sent our feet along that path He knew the side-lights should be burning still, and let us walk alone.

And then there is Circumstance. God closes things in around us till our alternatives are all reduced to one. That one, if we must act, is probably the will of God just then.

And then there are the Advice of others—an important element at least—and the Welfare of others, and the Example to others, and the many other facts and principles which make up the moral man, which, if not strong enough always to discover what God's will is, are not too feeble oftentimes to determine what it is *not*.

Even the best of these instruments, however, has but little power in its own hands. The ultimate appeal is always to the one great Instrument, which uses them in turn as it requires, and which supplements their discoveries, or even supplants them if it choose by its own superior light, and might, and right. It is like some great glass that can sweep the skies in the darkest night and trace the motions of the furthest stars, while all the rest can but see a faint uncertain light piercing for a moment here and there the clouds which lie between.

And this great instrument for finding out God's will, this instrument which can penetrate where reason cannot go, where observation has not been before, and memory is helpless, and the guiding hand of circumstance has failed, has a name which is seldom associated with any end so great, a name which every child may understand, even as the stupendous instrument itself with all its mighty powers is sometimes moved by infant hands when others have tried in vain.

The name of the instrument is Obedience. Obedience, as it is sometimes expressed, is the organ of spiritual knowledge. As the eye is the organ of physical sight; the mind, of intellectual sight; so the organ of spiritual vision is this strange power, Obedience.

This is one of the great discoveries the Bible has made to the world. It is purely a Bible thought. Philosophy never conceived a truth so simple and yet so sublime. And, although it was known in Old Testament times, and expressed in Old Testament books, it was reserved for Jesus Christ to make the full discovery to the world, and add to His teaching another of the profoundest truths which have come from heaven to earth—that the mysteries of the Father's will are hid in this word " obey."

The circumstances in which Christ made the great discovery to the world are known to every one.

The Feast of Tabernacles was in progress in Jerusalem when Jesus entered the temple to teach. A circle of Jews were gathered round Him who seem to have been spell-bound with the extraordinary wisdom of His words. He made no pretension to be a scholar. He was no graduate of the Rabbinical schools. He had no access to the sacred literature of the people. Yet here was this stranger from Nazareth confounding the wisest heads in Jerusalem, and unfolding with calm and effortless skill such truths as even these temple walls had never heard before. Then " the Jews marvelled, saying, ' How knoweth this man letters, never having learned ? ' " What organ of spiritual knowledge can He have, never having learned ? *Never having learned*—they did not know that Christ *had* learned. They did not know the school at Nazareth whose Teacher was in heaven—whose schoolroom was a carpenter's shop—the lesson, the Father's will. They knew not that hidden truths could come from God, or wisdom from above.

What came to them was gathered from human books, or caught from human lips. They knew no organ save the mind ; no instrument of knowing the things of heaven but that by which they learned in the schools. But Jesus points to a spiritual world which lay still far beyond, and tells them of the spiritual eye which reads its profounder secrets and reveals the mysteries of God. " My doctrine is not Mine," He says, " but His that sent Me " ; and " My judgment is just," as He taught before, " because I seek not Mine own will, but the will of the Father which hath sent Me." And then, lest men should think this great experience was never meant for them, He applies His principles to every human mind which seeks to know God's will. " If any man will do His will, he shall know of the doctrine, whether it be of God."

The word doctrine here is not to be taken in our sense of the word doctrine. It is not the doctrine of theology. " Any man " is to know if he will do His will. But it is God's teaching—God's mind. If any man will do His will, he shall know God's mind ; he shall know God's teaching and God's will.

In this sense, or indeed in the literal sense, from

the first look at these words it appears almost as if a contradiction were involved. To *know* God's will, it is as much as to say, *do* God's will. But how are we to *do* God's will *until* we know it? To *know* it; that is the very dilemma we are in. And it seems no way out of it to say, *Do* it and you shall *know* it. We want to know it, in order to do it; and now we are told to do it, in order to know it! If any man *do*, he shall *know*.

But that is not the meaning of the words. That is not even the words themselves. It is not, If any man *do*, he shall know; but if any man *will* do. And the whole sense of the passage turns upon that word *will*. It means, " If any man *is willing* to do, he shall know." He does not need to do His will in order to know, he only need be willing to do it. For " will " is not at all the sign of the future tense as it looks. It is not connected with the word *do* at all, but a separate verb altogether, meaning, " is willing," or " wills." If any man wills, or if any man is willing, to do, he shall know.

Now notice the difference this makes in the problem. Before, it looked as if the doing were to come first and then the knowing His will; but now another element is thrown in at the very beginning. The being willing comes first, and then the knowing; and thereafter the doing may follow—the doing, that is to say, if the will has been sufficiently clear to proceed.

The whole stress of the passage therefore turns on this word " will." And Christ's answer to the question, How to know the will of God ? may be simply stated thus : " If any man is willing to do God's will he shall know," or, in plainer language still, " If any man is sincerely trying to do God's will, he shall know."

The connection of all this with obedience is just that being willing is the highest form of obedience. It is the spirit and essence of obedience. There is an obedience in the world which is no obedience, because the act of obedience is there, but the spirit of submission is not.

" A certain man," we read in the Bible, " had two sons ; and he came to the first and said, ' Son, go work to-day in my vineyard.' He answered, ' I will not.' : but afterward he repented and went. And he came to the second, and said likewise. And he answered, ' I go, sir ' : and went not. Whether of them twain did the will of his father ? " Obedience here comes out in its true colours as a thing in the will. And if any man have an obeying will, a truly single and submissive will, he shall know of the teaching, or of the leading, whether it be of God.

If we were to carry out this principle into a practical case, it might be found to work in some such way as this. To-morrow, let us say, there is some difficulty before us in our path. It lies across the very threshold of our life, and we cannot begin the working week without, at least, some notice that it is there. It may be some trifling item of business life, over which unaccountable suspicions have begun to gather of late, and to force themselves in spite of everything into thought and conscience, and even into prayer. Or, it may be, some change of circumstance is opening up, and alternatives are appearing, and demanding choice of one. Perhaps it is some practice in our life, which the clearing of the spiritual atmosphere and increasing light from God are hinting to be wrong, while reason cannot coincide exactly and condemn. At all events there is something on the mind—something to do, to suffer, to renounce—and there are alternatives on the mind to distinguish, to choose from, to reject. Suppose, indeed, we made this case a personal as well as an illustrative thing, the question rises, How are we to separate God's light on the point from our own, disentangle our thoughts on the point from His, and be sure we are following His will, not the reflected image of ours ?

The first process towards this discovery naturally would be one of outlook. Naturally we would set to work by collecting all the possible materials for decision from every point of the compass, balancing the one consequence against the other, then summing up the points in favour of each by itself, until we chose the one which emerged at last with most of reason on its side. But this would only be the natural man's way out of the dilemma. The spiritual man would go about it in another way. This way, he would argue, has no religion in it at all, except perhaps the acknowledgment that reason is divine ; and though it might be quite possible and even probable that the light should come to him through the medium of reason, yet he would reach his conclusion, and likely enough a different conclusion, quite from another side.

And his conclusion would likewise be a better and sounder conclusion. For the insight of the non-religious method may be impaired, and the real organ of knowing God's will so out of order from disuse, that even reason would be biassed in its choice. A heart not quite subdued to God is an imperfect element, in which His will can never live ; and the intellect which belongs to such a heart is an imperfect instrument and cannot find

God's will unerringly—for God's will is found in regions which obedience only can explore.

Accordingly, he would go to work from the opposite side from the first. He would begin not in out-look, but in in-look. He would not give his mind to observation. He would devote his soul to self-examination, to self-examination of the most solemn and searching kind. For this principle of Christ is no concession to an easy life, or a careless method of rounding a difficult point. It is a summons rather to learn the highest and most sacred thing in Heaven, by bracing the heart to the loftiest and severest sacrifice on earth—the bending of an unwilling human will till it blends in the will of God. It means that the heart must be watched with a jealous care, and most solemnly kept for God. It means that the hidden desires must be taken out one by one and regenerated by Christ— that the faintest inclination of the soul, when touched by the spirit of God, must be prepared to assume the strength of will and act at any cost. It means that nothing in life should be dreaded so much as that the soul should ever lose its sensitiveness to God; that God should ever speak and find the ear just dull enough to miss what He has said; that God should have some active will for some human will to perform, and our heart be not the first in the world to be ready to obey.

When we have attained to this by meditation, by self-examination, by consecration, and by the Holy Spirit's power, we may be ready to make it our daily prayer, that we may know God's will ; and when the heart is prepared like this, and the wayward will is drilled in sacrifice and patience to surrender all to God, God's will may come out in our career at every turning of our life, and be ours not only in sacramental aspiration but in act.

To search for God's will with such an instrument is scarce to search at all. God's will lies transparently in view at every winding of the path ; and if perplexity sometimes comes, in such way as had been supposed, the mind will gather the phenomena into the field of vision, as carefully, as fully, as laboriously, as if no light would come at all, and then stand still and wait till the wonderful discerning faculty of the soul, that eye which beams in the undivided heart and looks right out to God from every willing mind, fixes its gaze on one far distant spot, one spot perhaps which is dark to all the world besides, where all the lights are focussed in God's will.

How this finite and this infinite are brought to

touch, how this invisible will of God is brought to the temporal heart must ever remain unknown. The mysterious meeting-place in the prepared and willing heart between the human and divine —where, precisely, the will is finally moved into line with God's—of these things knoweth no man save only the Spirit of God.

The wind bloweth where it listeth. " We hear the sound thereof, but cannot tell whence it cometh or whither it goeth." When every passion is annihilated, and no thought moves in the mind, and all the faculties are still and waiting for God, the spiritual eye may trace perhaps some delicate motion in the soul, some thought which stirs like a leaf in the unseen air and tells that God is there. It is not the stillness, nor the unseen breath, nor the thought that only stirred, but these three mysteries in one which reveal God's will to me. God's light, it is true, does not supersede, but illuminates our thoughts. Only when God sends an angel to trouble the pool let us have faith for the angel's hand, and believe that some power of Heaven has stirred the waters in our soul.

Let us but get our hearts in position for knowing the will of God—only let us be willing to know God's will in our hearts that we may do God's will in our lives, and we shall raise no questions as to

how this will may come, and feel no fears in case
the heavenly light should go.

But let it be remembered, as already said, that
it requires a well-kept life to will to do this will.
It requires a well-kept life to *do* the will of God,
and even a better kept life to *will* to do His will.
To be willing is a rarer grace than to be doing the
will of God. For he who is willing may sometimes
have nothing to do, and must only be willing to
wait : and it is easier far to be doing God's will
than to be willing to have nothing to do—it is
easier far to be working for Christ than it is to be
willing to cease. No, there is nothing rarer in the
world to-day than the truly willing soul, and there
is nothing more worth coveting than the will to
will God's will. There is no grander possession for
any Christian life than the transparently simple
mechanism of a sincerely obeying heart. And if
we could keep the machinery clear, there would
be lives in thousands doing God's will on earth
even as it is done in Heaven. There would be God
in many a man's career whose soul is allowed to
drift—a useless thing to God and the world—with
every changing wind of life, and many a noble
Christian character rescued from wasting all its
virtues on itself and saved for work for Christ.

And when the time of trial comes, and all in

earth and heaven is dark and even God's love seems
dim : what is there ever left to cling to but this
will of the willing heart, a God-given, God-ward
bending will, which says amidst the most solemn
and perplexing vicissitudes of life :

" Father, I know that all my life
   Is portioned out for me ;
The changes that are sure to come
   I do not fear to see ;
I ask Thee for a present mind,
   Intent on pleasing Thee."

V.

THE
RELATION OF THE WILL OF GOD
TO SANCTIFICATION

THE RELATION OF THE WILL OF GOD
TO SANCTIFICATION

" This is the will of God, even your sanctification."
—1 THESS. iv. 3.

" As He which hath called you is holy, so be ye
holy in all manner of conversation ; because it is
written, ' Be ye holy, for I am holy.' "—1 PET.
i. 15, 16.

" Lo, I come to do Thy will, O God. . . . By the
which will we are sanctified through the offering
of the body of Jesus Christ once for all."—
HEB. x. 9, 10.

OUR discussion of the will of God landed us—
perhaps in rather an unforeseen way—in the great
subject of sanctification. You may remember that
we made this discovery, that the end of sanctification, in the sense of consecration, is to do the
will of God, and that the proof was based on these
words : " Present your bodies a living sacrifice,
holy, acceptable unto God, and be not conformed
to this world." Why ? " That ye may prove what
is that good and acceptable and perfect will of

God." We are to present ourselves to God, not because it is a pleasant and luxurious thing to live in the state of consecration, but to do the will of God. Or, to sum this up in a single sentence, it might read : " This is sanctification, even to prove the will of God."

But our text to-day is apparently the very opposite to this. " This is the will of God, even your sanctification." Then it looked as if sanctification was in order to the will of God ; now it looks as if the will of God was in order to sanctification.

It is evident, therefore, that there is still something in this part of the subject which demands a clearance. And in order to gain this it will be necessary to present the other side of the same question, and complete the view of the subject of holiness itself.

There are in the Bible two great meanings to the word sanctification. The first may be roughly called the Old Testament word. The second is identified, but not exclusively, with the New. The Old Testament meaning had this peculiarity, that it did not necessarily imply any inward change in the heart sanctified. In fact, it was not even necessarily applied to hearts at all, but to things. A field could be sanctified, a house could be sanctified, an altar, a tabernacle, gold and silver vessels, the garments of the priest, the cities of refuge. Anything, in short, that was set apart for sacred use was said to be *sanctified*. But the New Testament word had a deeper meaning. It meant not only outward consecration, but inward holiness. It meant an internal purification of the heart from all uncleanness, and an enduing it with the mind of Christ. It was not a mere separation like the first, but a visitation—a separation from the lower world, and a visitation from the higher, the coming in of God's Spirit from above with a principle of holiness that was to work an inward likeness to the character of God.

The practical object of the first process is mainly to put the thing in position where God can use it. A golden candlestick was sanctified, so that it might be of some use to God. A house was sanctified, so that it might be exclusively His—to do what He liked with. In like manner a man is consecrated—that God may use him. It is the process by which he is got into position for God. And all that sanctification does for him, in the first sense of the word, is so to put him in position that he shall always be within reach of God—that he shall do what God likes, do, that is to say, what God wills.

But there is something more in sanctification than man's merely being a tool in the hands of God. If there were not, automatons could do the work far better than men. They would never oppose God's will, and they would always be in position. But God's will has a reaction upon the instruments whom He employs. God's will does not stop with His will, as it were. It recoils back upon the person using it, and benefits him If the instrument is a sanctified cup, or a sanctified house, it does not recoil back, and make an internal change in them ; but if it is a person who does God's will, God's will is not only done, but the person or doer is affected. God never keeps anything all to Himself He who so loved the world that He gave His only begotten Son, does He not with Him also freely give us all things ? His Son is for us, His love is for us, His will is for us. How do we know that it is for us ? Because this is the will of God, even your sanctification. Whatever else may be involved in it, this is in it ; whatever else He may get from it, this is something which you get, your sanctification " By the which will," as Hebrews says, " we are sanctified." " This is My will, not My gain, but yours ; not My eternal advantage, but yours ; not My holiness, but ' your sanctification ' " Do you think God wants your body when He asks you to present it to Him ? Do you think it is for His sake that He asks it, that He might be enriched by it ? God could make a thousand better with a breath. It is for your sake He asks it He wants your gift to give you His gift—your gift which was just in the way of His gift. He wants your will out of the way, to make room for His will. You give everything to God. God gives it all back again, and more. You present your body a living sacrifice that you may prove God's will. You shall prove it by getting back your body—a glorified body. You lose the world that you may prove God's will. God's will is that you shall gain heaven. This is the will of God, therefore, that you should gain heaven. Or this is the will of God that you should gain holiness, for holiness is heaven. Or this is the will of God, even your sanctification.

To sum up these facts, then, we find that they shape themselves into these two propositions :—

1. That our sanctification, or more strictly, our consecration, is in order to the will of God, " to prove what is that good and acceptable and perfect will of God."

2. That this reacts upon ourselves—a conspicuous part of God's will being that we should be personally holy. " This is the will of God, even your sanctification."

The first of these has already been discussed, and now the question comes to be how we can best fulfil this conspicuous part of the will of God and become holy ourselves. It is God's will for all of us that we should become holy. How are we to become holy ?

We have probably asked this question many times already in our life. We have thought and read, and prayed about it, and perhaps have never yet reached the conclusion how indeed we are to become holy. Perhaps the question has long ago assumed another and evasive form with us, " When are we going to become holy ? " or perhaps a hopeless form, " How *ever* are we to become holy ? "

Now the real way out of the difficulty is to ask a deeper question still : " Why do I want to be holy ? " All the great difficulties of religion are centred round our motives. Impurities in a spiritual stream generally mean impurities at the spiritual source. And all fertility or barrenness of soul depends upon which source supplies the streams of the desires. Our difficulties about becoming holy, therefore, most likely lie in our reasons for wishing to become holy. For if you grant the true motive to holiness, you need no definition of holiness. True holiness lies in touching the true motive. We shall get nearer the true roots of holiness, therefore, if we spend a little time over the root question : " Why do I wish to be holy ? "

1. The first thing which started some of us to search for a better life, perhaps, was *Infection*. We caught an infection for a better life from some one we knew. We were idling our own way through life, when some one crossed our path—some one with high aims and great enthusiasms. We were taken with the principles on which that life was lived. Its noble purpose charmed us : its disregards of the petty troubles and cares of life astonished us. We felt unaccountably interested in it. There was a romance in its earnestness and self-denial that captivated us, and we thought we should like to take down our own life, and put it together again on this new plan. So we got our first motive to holiness

Now this was not a wrong motive—it was only an imperfect one. It answered its purpose—so far. For God takes strange ways to start a man's religion. There is nothing more remarkable in the history of conversion, for instance, than the infinite diversity of answers to this question : " What made you first think about your soul ? " God does take strange ways to start a man for heaven. The way home is sometimes shown him by an unexpected finger-post ; and from a motive so unworthy that he dare not tell it in after-life, there comes to many a man his first impulse toward God. And long after he has begun to run the Christian race, God may try to hasten his lagging steps by the spur of a motive as far beneath an heir of heaven as his spiritual life is beneath what it ought to be.

But the principle to be noted through it all is this, that the motives which God allows us to start on are the ones we are to live on. It may be adversity in business that gives us a fresh start. It may be affliction, or ambition, or church-pride, or a thousand things. But such an impulse cannot last, and it cannot carry us far. And there must come a time to exchange it for a higher one if we would grow in grace, or move onward into a holier life. A man's motive must grow, if grace would grow. And many a man has to live on old grace, because he lives on an old motive. God let us begin with a lower one, and then when He gave us more grace, it was that we might get a higher one ; but we spent the grace on something else, and our motive is no higher than before. So, although we got a start in religion, we were little the better for it, and our whole life has stood still for want of a strong enough motive to go on.

2. But it was not necessary that we should have caught our infection from a friend. There is another

great source of infection, and some of us are breathing its atmosphere every day—*books*. We may have got our motives to be good from a book. We found in works on ethics, and in all great poets, and even perhaps in some novels, that the highest aim of life was to be true and pure and good. We found modern literature ringing with the praises of virtue. By-and-by we began to respect it, then to admire it, then to wish for it. Thus we caught the enthusiasm for purity which has changed our whole lives, in a way, and given us a chief motive to religion.

Well, we must thank God for having given us a start, anyhow. It is something to have begun. It is a great thing to have an enthusiasm to be true and pure and good. Nor will the Bible ever be jealous of any lesser book which God may use to stir men up to a better life. But all lesser books sin and come short. And the greatest motives of the greatest of the lesser books fall as far short of the glory of God as those who live only by the enthusiasms which are kindled on the altar of modern literature fall short of the life and mind of Christ. God may give these motives to a man to start with. If he will not look into God's Book for them, God may see fit to put something remotely like them into men's books. Jesus Christ used to come to

men where they were. There is no place on earth
so dark that the light of heaven will not come to
it ; and there is no spot on earth where God may
not choose to raise a monument of His love. There
is always room anywhere in the world for a holy
thought. It may come to a man on the roadside,
as to Paul ; or in the fork of a sycamore tree, as
to Zacchæus. It may come to him at his boats,
as to Peter ; or at his Bible, as to the Eunuch.
But, whether it come at the boats, or whether
it come at the Bible, whatever is good is God's ;
and men may be thankful that the Giver of all
good has peopled the whole earth and air and sky
with thoughts of His glory, and filled the world
with voices which call men near to Him. At the
same time, it must be understood again that the
initial motives are never meant to continue us far
on the road to God. As a matter of fact, they never
can continue us ; and if a man does not get higher
ones, his religion must, and his morality may,
come to a bitter end. The melancholy proof occurs
to every one in a moment, that those who inspire
us with these almost Divine enthusiasms are, and
have been, many of them, degraded men and women
themselves. For if a man's motives to goodness
are not higher than the enthusiasms of his own
higher nature, the chances are that the appeals

of his lower nature, in time, will either curb or degrade them.

The true motive to holiness, then, is not to be caught from books.

3. In the next place, some of us, perhaps, were induced to aim at a better life from *prudential motives*, or from *fear*.

We had read in the Bible a very startling sentence —" Without holiness no man shall see the Lord." Now we wished to see God. And we found the Bible full of commands to keep God's law. So, with fear and trembling, we began to try. Its strictness was a continual stimulus to us. We were kept watching and praying. We lived in an atmosphere of fear, lest we should break it. No doubt this has done good—great good. Like the others, it was not a bad motive—only an imperfect one. But, like the others, it will have to be exchanged for a higher one, if true progress in holy living is to be made.

4. Then some of us found another motive in *gratitude*. The great love of God in Christ had come home to us with a peculiar power. We felt the greatness of His sacrifice for us, of His forgiveness of us. And we would try to return His love. So we set our hearts with a gracious purpose towards God. Our life and conversation should be becoming

the Gospel of Christ. We would do for His sake
what we would never do for our own sake. But
even a noble impulse like this has failed to fulfil
our heart's desire, and even our generosity has
left us little nearer God

5 And, lastly, there is this other thought
which has sometimes helped us onward for a
time—a feeling which comes over us at Communion times, at revival times, which Christian
workers feel at all times : "Here are we sur-
rounded by great privileges—singled out from the
world for God's peculiar care. God comes very
close to us ; the very ground is holy oftentimes.
What manner of persons ought we to be in holy
conversation and godliness ; How different we
ought to be from all the people around ! How much
more separate from every appearance of evil !
How softly we should walk, who bear the vessels
of the Lord ! "

Now some of these motives are very beautiful
They are the gifts of God. Doubtless many have
attained to a certain measure of holiness by em-
ploying them. And they have at least awakened
in us some longings after God. But they are all
deficient, and hopelessly inadequate to carry on
what sometimes they so hopefully begin.

And they are deficient in these three ways :—

1. They are unscriptural—rather, they do not convey the full scriptural truth.

2. They are inadequate to produce more than a small degree of holiness.

3. They never produce the true quality of holiness.

If we have not yet had higher motives than these, then it follows that our spiritual life is being laid down upon principles which can never in the nature of things yield the results we had hoped and waited for

We have been wondering why our growth in grace has been so small—so small, indeed, that sometimes it has almost seemed to cease. And as we look into our hearts, we find this one reason, at least—perhaps the great one—that our *motive* is incomplete

Now, the weakness of the old motive, apart from the error of it, consisted in this : in the first place it wanted authority ; in the second, it proposed no standard. As regards the first, there was no reason why one should strive to be better. It was left to one's own discretion. Our friend said it, or our favourite author, and the obligation rose or fell with the nearness or remoteness of their influence. And as regards the standard, our friend or our favourite author's favourite hero was but a poor model at the best, for only a most imperfect spiritual beauty can ever be copied from anything made of clay.

Well, then, what is the right motive to holiness of life ? We have been dealing with ordinary motives hitherto ; now we must come to extra-ordinary ones. Holiness is one of the most extra-ordinary things in life, and it demands the noblest motives, the noblest impulses, or none. Now we shall see how God has satisfied this demand of our nature for an extraordinary motive to this extra-ordinary thing, holiness—satisfied it so completely, that the soul, when it finds it out, need never feel unsatisfied again. God's motive to holiness is, " *Be ye holy, for I am holy.*"

It is a startling thing when the voice of God comes close to us and whispers, " Be ye holy " ; but when the question returns from our lips, " Why should we be holy " ? it is a more solemn thing to get this answer, " For I am holy." This is God's motive to holiness—" For I am holy." *Be ye holy* : here is its authority—its Divine obligation. *For I am holy*—here is its Divine motive.

Be ye holy. Think of the greatness of the obligation. Long ago, when we began the Christian

life, we heard a voice, " Be ye holy." Perhaps, as
we have seen it, it was an infectious voice, the voice
of a friend. Perhaps it was an inspiring voice, the
voice of poetry and literature. Perhaps it was a
warning voice, the voice of the law. But it was
not a commanding voice—the voice of God. And
the reason was, perhaps, that we were not thinking
of the voice : we were thinking of the " holy."
We had caught sight of a new and beautiful
object—something which seemed full of promise,
which was to consecrate even the common hours
of our life. The religious world seemed bright to
us then, and the books and the men were dear
that would help us to reach out our hands to this.
It was something new that had come into our life
—this fascination of holiness. Had we been asked
about the voice which said, "Be ye holy," we should
indeed have said it was God's. But, in truth, it
was only our own voice, which had caught some
far-off echoes from our reading, or our thinking,
or our friends. There was no authority in the voice,
therefore, and it rested with our own poor wills
whether we should grow in holiness or not. Sometimes our will was strong, and we were better
men and women then than ever in our lives
before ; but there were intervals when we listened
to another voice, " Be ye prosperous," or " Be

ye happy," and then we lost all we had gained.

But with the Divine obligation before us, it is no longer optional that we should be holy. We must be holy. And then see how the motive to holiness is attached to the obligation to holiness— the motive for holiness : *" For I am holy "* The motive accounts for the obligation. God's one desire for the whole earth is that it should be holy—just because He is holy. And the best He can do with men is to make them like Himself. The whole earth is His, and He would have it all in harmony with Him. God has a right to demand that we should be holy—that every one should be holy, and everything, just because He is holy Himself. To take even the lowest ground, we allow no ornaments in our house that are not lovely and pleasant to the eye. We have no business to cumber God's earth with ourselves if we are not holy—no business to live in the same world with Him. We are an offence to God—discordant notes in the music of the universe

But God lays this high obligation upon us for our own sake. For this we were made For this we were born in a Christian land. For this, strange things have happened in our lives—strange pieces of discipline have disturbed their quiet flow, strange troubles, strange providences, strange chastenings. There is no other explanation of the mystery of our life than this, that God would have us holy. At any cost God will have us holy. Whatever else we may be, this one thing we *must* be. This is the will of God, even our sanctification. It is not necessary that we should be prosperous or famous, or happy. But it is necessary that we should be holy ; and the deepest moments of our lives give us glimpses sometimes of a more tender reason still why God says, " Be ye holy "— it is for our own sakes : because it would be hell to be unholy.

There is now only one thing wanting in our new motive to holiness. We have discovered the sources of its obligation far up in the counsels of God, and deep down in the weakness of our own nature. We have found holiness to be an absolutely necessary virtue—to live without which is to contradict our Maker. But we have not yet looked at its *quality*. The thing we are to pursue so ardently—what is it ? How are we to shape it to ourselves when we think of it ? Is there any plain definition of it—any form which could be easily stated and easily followed It may be very easily stated It is for those who have tried it to say whether it be easily followed. Be ye holy, *as* He is holy. *As* He is holy, as He who hath called you is holy, *so* be ye holy. This is the form of holiness we are asked to aim at. This is the standard, God's commentary on the motive. " As He . . . so ye." Ponder for a moment the difference between these pronouns. *He—Ye. He* who hath called you—Jesus Christ. *He* who did no sin, neither was guile found in his mouth. *He* who when He was reviled, reviled not again, when He suffered, He threatened not. *He* who was without spot or blemish, in whom even His enemies found no fault.

Ye the fallen children of a fallen race. *Ye* with hearts deceitful above all things, and desperately wicked. *Ye* are to become as *He.* The two pronouns are to approach one another. The crucifiers are to work their way up to the crucified. *Ye* are to become as *He.* Here is a motive as high as the holiness of God. It makes us feel as if we had our life-work before us still. We have scarcely even begun to be like God—for we began perhaps with no higher motive than to be like some one else—not like God at all. But the little betterness that we get from books, the chance impulses that come from other lives, have never fulfilled in us the will of God—could never sanctify such hearts as ours, and make *ye* become as *He.*

No doubt a great deal of human good is possible to man before he touches the character of Christ. High human motives and human aims may make a noble human life. But they never make a holy life. A holy life is a life like Christ's. And whatever may be got from the lower motives to a better life, one thing must necessarily be absent from them all—the life like Christ's, or rather, the spirit like Christ's. For the life like Christ's can only come from Christ ; and the spirit of Christ can only be caught from Christ

Hence, therefore, we come at last to the profound meaning of another text which stands alone in the Word of God, and forms the only true climax to such a subject as this.

"Lo, I come to do Thy will, O God," the author of the Hebrews quotes from David, and goes on to add, "*By the which will we are sanctified.*" Christ came to do God's will, by the which will we are sanctified. This is the will of God, even your sanctification. But the writer of the Hebrews adds another lesson : "By the which will we are sanctified." How ? "Through the offering of the body of Jesus Christ once for all." Our sanctification is not in books, or in noble enthusiasm, or in personal struggles after a better life. It is in the offering of the body of Jesus Christ once for all. Justification is through the blood of Jesus Christ once for all. Sanctification is through the body of Jesus Christ once for all. It is not a thing to be generated, but to be received. It is not to be generated in fragments of experience at one time and another—it is already complete in Christ. We have only to put on Christ. And though it may take a lifetime of experience to make it ours, the sanctification, whenever it come, can only come from Christ, and if we ever are sanctified it will only be because, and inasmuch as we have Christ. Our sanctification is not what morality gives, not even what the Bible gives, not even what Christ gives, it is what Christ *lives*. It is Christ Himself.

The reason why we resort so much to lower impulses to a Christian life is imperfect union with Christ. We take our doctrines from the Bible and our assurance from Christ, but for want of the living bright reality of His presence in our hearts we search the world all round for impulses. We search religious books for impulses, and tracts and sermons, but in vain. They are not there. " I am Alpha and Omega, the beginning and the end." " Christ is all and in all." The beginning of all things is in the will of God. The end of all things is in sanctification through faith in Jesus

Christ. " By the which will ye are sanctified."
Between these two poles all spiritual life and
Christian experience run. And no motive outside
Christ can lead a man to Christ. If your motive
to holiness is not as high as Christ it cannot make
you rise to Christ. For water cannot rise above
its level. " Beware, therefore, lest any man spoil
you through philosophy and vain deceit, after the
tradition of men, after the rudiments of the world,
and not after Christ. For in Him dwelleth all the
fulness of the Godhead bodily. And ye are complete in Him which is the head of all principality
and power " (Col. ii. 8–10). " Who of God is made
unto us wisdom and righteousness, and sanctification and redemption " (1 Cor. i. 30). " *As* ye
have therefore received the Lord Jesus *so* walk
ye *in Him*."